A First Drawing Book

RHINOCEROS CAN'T DRAW

But YOU can!

I can skateboard, though!

Noodle Juice Ltd
www.noodle-juice.com
Stonesfield House, Stanwell Lane, Great Bourton, Oxfordshire, OX17 1QS
First published in Great Britain 2023
Copyright © Noodle Juice Ltd 2023
Text by Luke Newell and Noodle Juice 2022
Illustrations by Luke Newell and Mr Griff 2022
All rights reserved
Printed in China
A CIP catalogue record of this book is available from the British Library.
ISBN: 978-1-915613-13-4
3 5 7 9 10 8 6 4 2

This book is made from FSC®-certified paper. By choosing this book, you help to take care of the world's forests. Learn more: www.fsc.org.

Words, words, words. All useless, darling... Art is the mirror of the soul.

Rhinoceros can't draw, but YOU can!

Contents

4	Anyone Can Draw!	
6	Getting Started	
8	Top Tip #1:	Drawing Straight Lines
10	Top Tip #2:	Drawing Circles
11	Big Idea #1:	Light and Shade
18	Top Tip #3:	Thumb Measuring
20	Big Idea #2:	Perspective
26	Warm-up #1:	Two-minute Triples
28	Big Idea #3:	Light, Shade and Perspective Combined, or Not...
32	Warm-up #2:	Verb Noun Raffle
34	Big Idea #4:	People
39	Top Tip #4:	Shadows
42	Warm-up #3:	Blind Drawing
40	Top Tip #5:	Hands
44	Big Idea #5:	Human Faces
52	Top Tip #6:	Line-edge Quality
54	Big Idea #6:	Animals
60	Warm-up #4:	One-line Drawing
62	Big Idea #7:	Vehicles
66	Warm-up #5:	Quick Draw
68	Big Idea #8:	Buildings
72	Warm-up #6:	Scribble Monsters
74	Big Idea #9:	Nature
78	Warm-up #7:	Just Use Tone
80	Big Idea #10:	Landscapes
84	So Can You Draw?	
86	Perspective Grids	
88	Practice Pages	
95	Index	

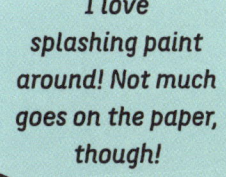

I love splashing paint around! Not much goes on the paper, though!

I'm going to need all your help!

Anyone Can Draw!

The biggest thing that stops anyone from drawing is fear. 'What if it doesn't look good? – I don't have a PERFECT idea. – My mind's gone blank!' The best way to overcome that fear is to go with the BIG IDEA!

This book is all about those BIG IDEAS – the BIG PRINCIPLES of drawing. Once you – and Rhinoceros – have learned the rules, all you have to do is GIVE IT A TRY!

There are 10 BIG IDEAS in this book.

Each idea has several different fill-in activities for you to work through. There are also TOP TIPS and WARM-UP EXERCISES that will help you perfect your new artistic skills.

Meet the team

Tiger

Artist in residence. Can be a little dramatic.

Orangutan

The art expert. Orangutan has plenty of advice to help you become an artist.

Your job as an artist is to decide what to show and what not to show!

Rhinoceros

Has a lot to learn!

I like drawing with sticks ... also handy for dental hygiene.

Crocodile

Tends to make a mess and is always hungry!

LOTS OF PEOPLE THINK 'I CAN'T DRAW!' but if you know the alphabet, you already know 26 ... no, 52 unique symbols that express something.

Aa Bb Cc Dd Ee Ff Gg

When you draw, you use the same hand and the same pencil as you do when you write. In fact, people have been making pictures for much longer than they have used letters.

The alphabet actually started off as pictures. The letter A was a cow's head (Aleph), the letter B was a house (Beth). So if you can write, you'll be able to draw.

To learn how, follow the big ideas, have fun completing the activities and then you – and hopefully Rhinoceros – will be an artist in no time.

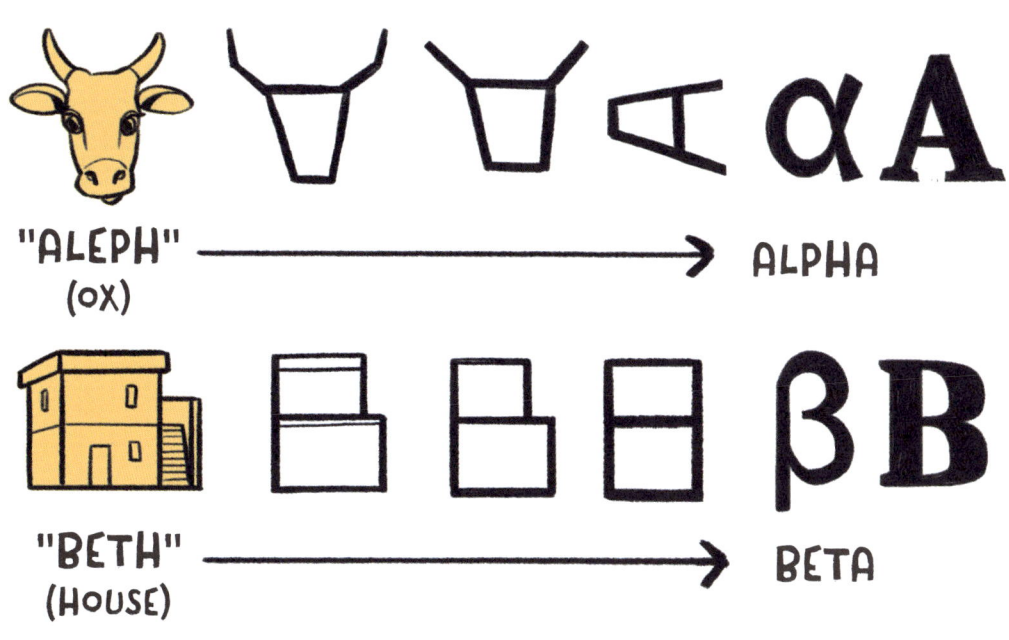

"ALEPH" (OX) ⟶ ALPHA

"BETH" (HOUSE) ⟶ BETA

Drawing is as easy as Aa Bb Cc!

Getting Started

Drawing is just mark making. We can make LINES – straight lines, curved lines, clean lines or scraggly lines! Or we can make areas of TONE – flat blocks of either dark or light. That's it! Drawing is really just playing with these things.

What you will need

You don't need any special equipment, just paper to draw on and something to draw with.

The artist (that's you!) creates the artwork and while there is lots of lovely equipment and materials out there, 'better stuff' doesn't always make better art.

You can scratch something beautiful in a muddy puddle with a stick, BUT some things are handy to have while completing the activities in this book.

Soft(ish) pencils

Pencils are great to draw with. They let you change the LINE QUALITY from thin to thick, faint to dark. Sketch lightly and loosely while working things out, then go in darker, more precisely, once you're happy. You can even use the pencil angled to fill in blocks of TONE.

Colour pencils

Colour pencils are GREAT as they're usually quite soft. Use a light-coloured pencil when you're working things out. Then go over the top with a darker colour to create the finished piece.

An exercise book or loose sheets of paper

It's a good idea to work on loose paper as it's useful to be able to ROTATE your page (see page 8), or stick bits together if you need to.

A mirror

Just a small make-up mirror is very useful ... mainly for when you want to draw a facial expression, but also for sneakily drawing things or people BEHIND you!

Your own body

Getting up and actually pulling the pose or making the facial expression is REALLY IMPORTANT. You can FEEL which muscles are engaging, feel the stretch of clothing across your body – where does the weight go? You may think you LOOK SILLY, but you're an ARTIST, embrace the silliness and it will make the drawing better.

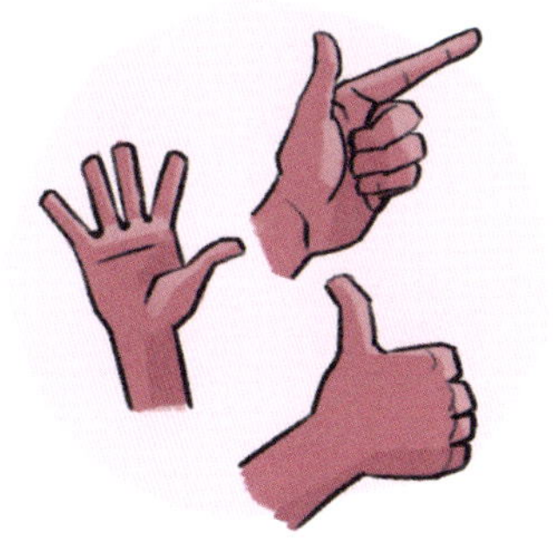

An eraser

Use an eraser if you like, but it can be helpful to keep the mistakes in there! You can look back and see HOW you built up your picture.

A ruler?

Rulers are useful, but sometimes ruler-drawn lines can stop the FLOW, and make your drawing look stiff. Mostly in art, lines don't have to be RULER PERFECT, even when doing TECHNICAL STUFF like perspective (Big Idea #2). Practise drawing straight lines without a ruler on the next page.

TOP TIP #1 Drawing Straight Lines

Practise drawing straight lines, 'freehand'...

Put a dot where you want the line to start and another dot where you want the line to end.

Hovering above the paper, without putting the pencil on it, do some practice SWOOSHES between the dots.

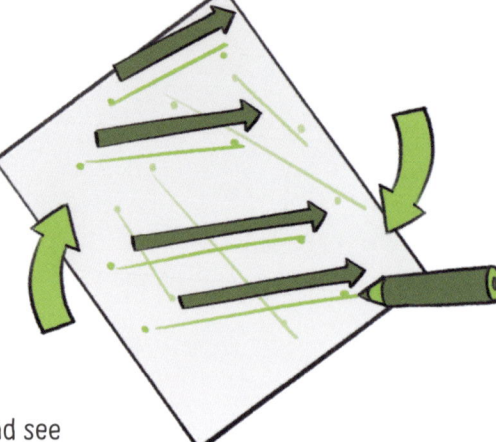

When you're ready, do three more swooshes! On the third one, put the pencil on the paper and draw the line. Did you hit both dots?

Draw lots of dots, and see how close you can get! Nobody can draw a perfect straight line (you're not a robot and that's GOOD!) but you will get good at straight lines pretty fast. Use the space on the next page to practise.

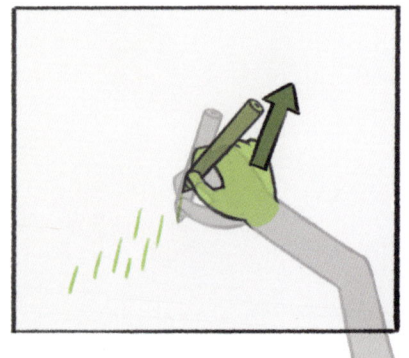

Draw shorter lines from the wrist, longer lines from your elbow and ginormous lines from your shoulder.

Your lines will tend to be thicker at the end of the stroke than they are at the beginning.

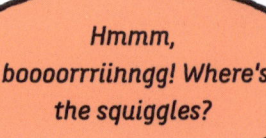

Hmmm, boooorrriinngg! Where's the squiggles?

Turn the paper so your wrist is straight and comfortable for swooshing from your elbow!

I like turning the page until I've made a box. Or a triangle. I like triangles!

TOP TIP #2 Drawing Circles

Now try circles...

Start swooshing in circles above the paper. When you're ready, put the pencil on the page and keep circling.

Drawing from your fingers or wrist will result in smaller circles. Drawing from your elbow, or even shoulder, will create bigger circles and longer curves. You might need a bigger piece of paper, but use the space opposite to practise some small circles.

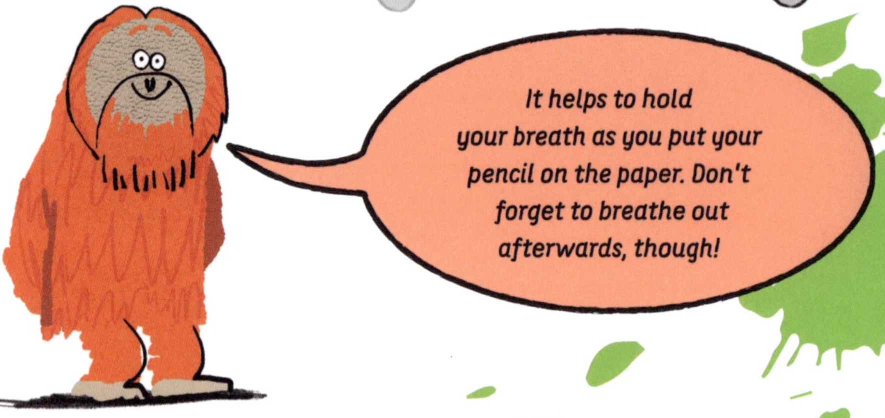

It helps to hold your breath as you put your pencil on the paper. Don't forget to breathe out afterwards, though!

I like drawing egg shapes too.

Darling, I think you'll find the correct term for an egg shape is an ellipse.

10

BIG IDEA #1 Light and Shade

The first BIG IDEA is that THE VISIBLE WORLD IS JUST LIGHT AND SHADE. Artists use TONE to replicate how light and shadow falls across 3D objects. You can choose a TONAL RANGE for your drawing, or it might be steered by the tonal range of the pen or pencil you are using.

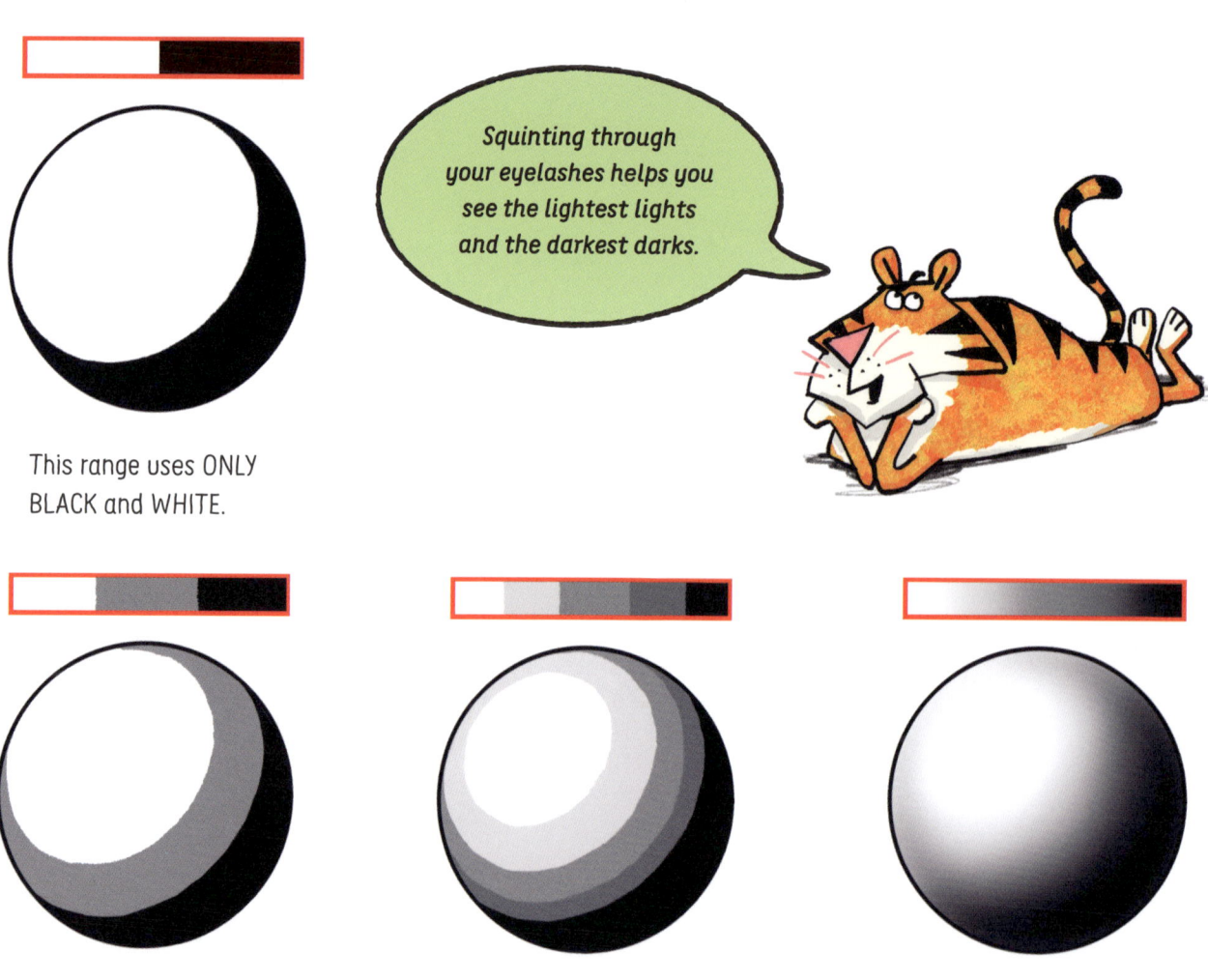

Squinting through your eyelashes helps you see the lightest lights and the darkest darks.

This range uses ONLY BLACK and WHITE.

This range uses BLACK, WHITE and a MIDTONE.

This one has two more distinct tones. Let's call them MID-MIDTONES.

This last one uses the whole range!

When drawing, you are always bookended by the darkest dark and the lightest light. Everything in between is up to you. Why don't you have a try?

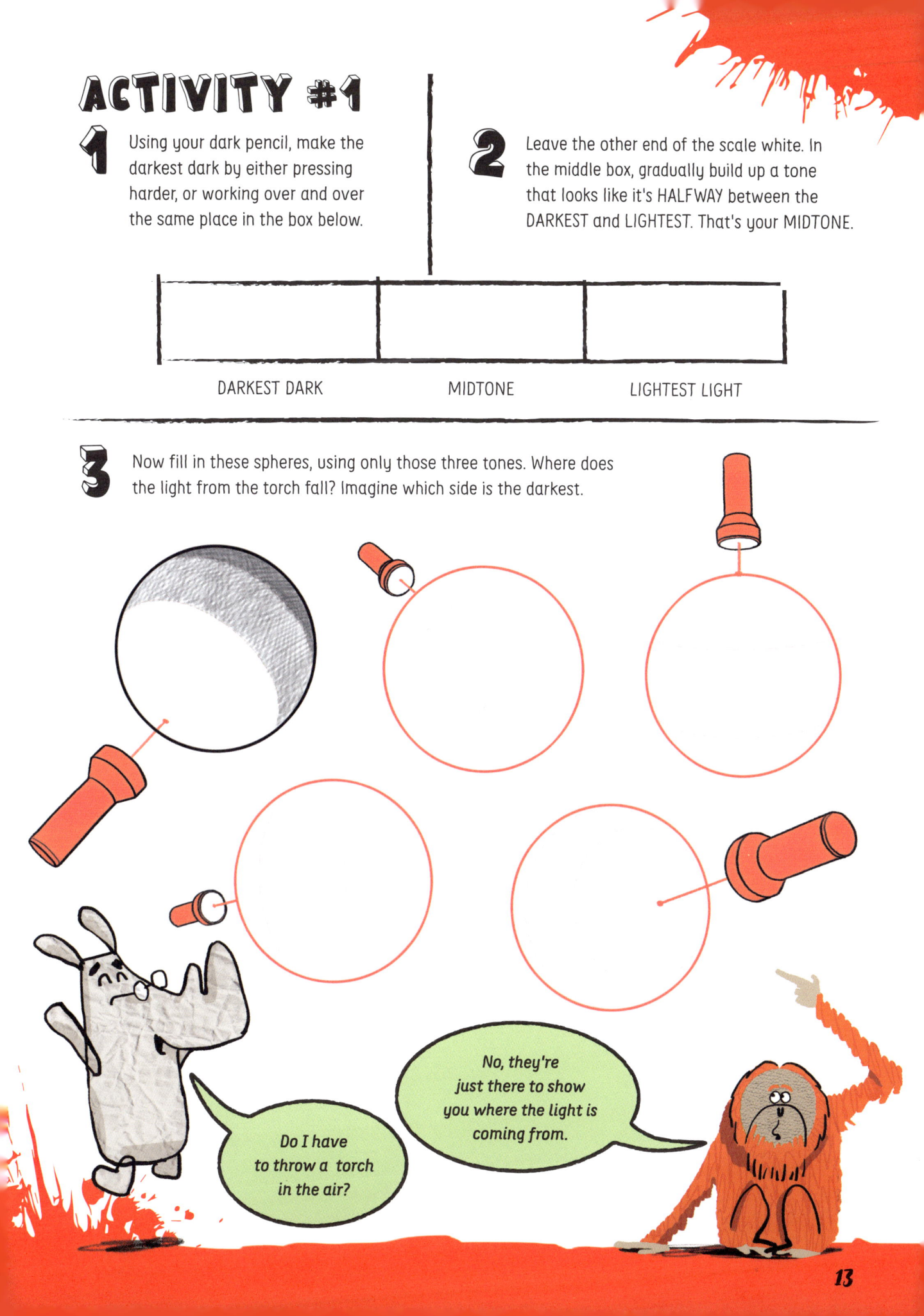

ACTIVITY #1

1 Using your dark pencil, make the darkest dark by either pressing harder, or working over and over the same place in the box below.

2 Leave the other end of the scale white. In the middle box, gradually build up a tone that looks like it's HALFWAY between the DARKEST and LIGHTEST. That's your MIDTONE.

DARKEST DARK   MIDTONE   LIGHTEST LIGHT

3 Now fill in these spheres, using only those three tones. Where does the light from the torch fall? Imagine which side is the darkest.

Do I have to throw a torch in the air?

No, they're just there to show you where the light is coming from.

13

ACTIVITY #2

It's time to add in two more tones, the MID-MIDTONES!

1 Take your dark pencil and fill in the section labellled DARKEST DARK. Leave the opposite end white and fill in your midtone.

2 Now, fill in the gaps. Take MID-MIDTONE #1 slightly darker than your midtone, and MID-MIDTONE #2 slightly lighter – approximately halfway between the two tones either side.

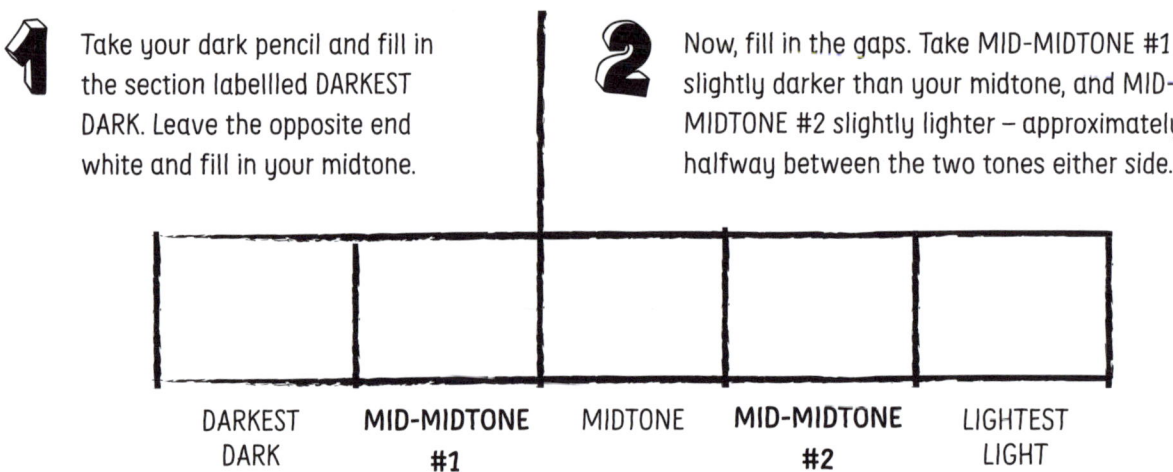

| DARKEST DARK | **MID-MIDTONE #1** | MIDTONE | **MID-MIDTONE #2** | LIGHTEST LIGHT |

3 These spheres have the same light sources as the spheres in Activity #1. Where can you use your MID-MIDTONES now?

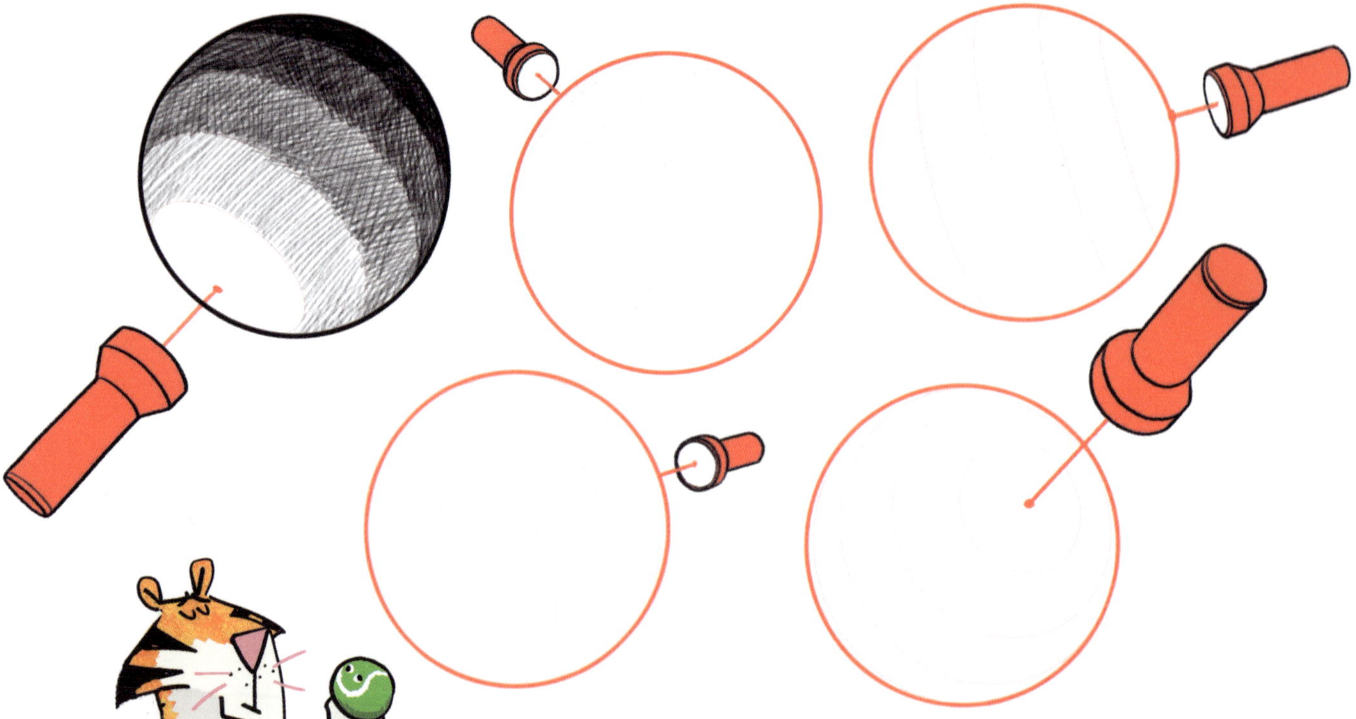

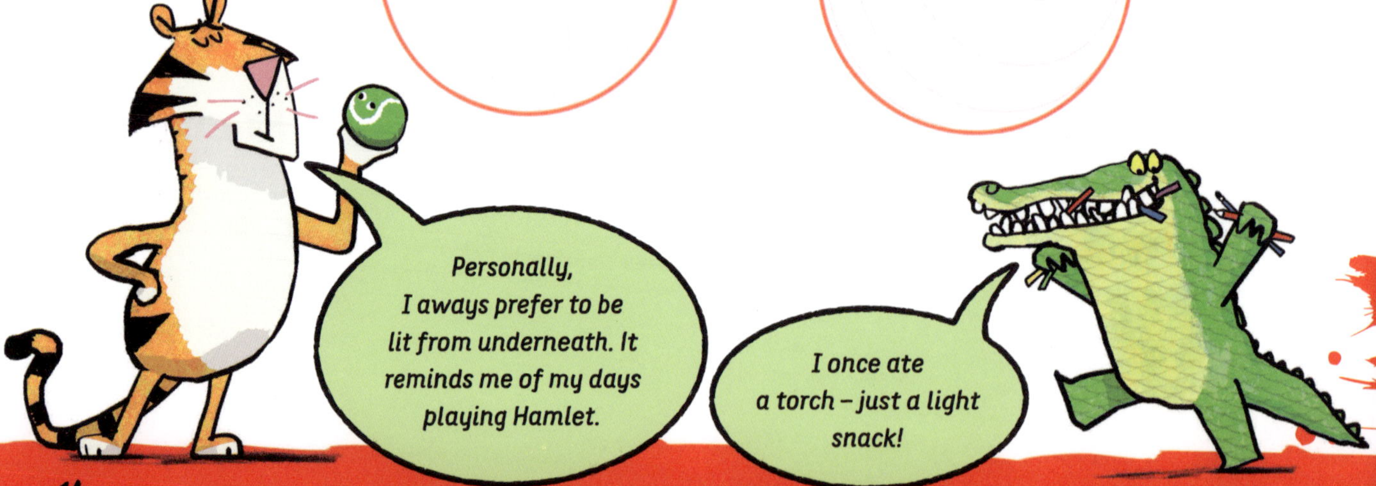

Personally, I aways prefer to be lit from underneath. It reminds me of my days playing Hamlet.

I once ate a torch – just a light snack!

Try using your five different tones to finish shading this simple scene. Think about where the light is coming from and where the darkest dark and lightest light areas would be.

> Remember to use your eyes and really study what you're drawing. Look around you. Can you see other objects with similar lighting? How do their shadows look?

ACTIVITY #3

This activity uses the whole range of tones! Even though we're not separating them into DISTINCT tones, you start the same way.

1 Fill in your darkest dark, leave the opposite end white and find your midtone.

2 Then BLEND between the different tones to find your whole tonal range. You can use the side of your pencil to cover the area more quickly.

DARKEST DARK — MIDTONE — LIGHTEST LIGHT

3 Try putting some light and shade on to these objects. It can be less obvious what to do with soft edges or curvy shapes, but start with where you think the darkest dark would fall. Then decide the lightest areas and colour in the midtones.

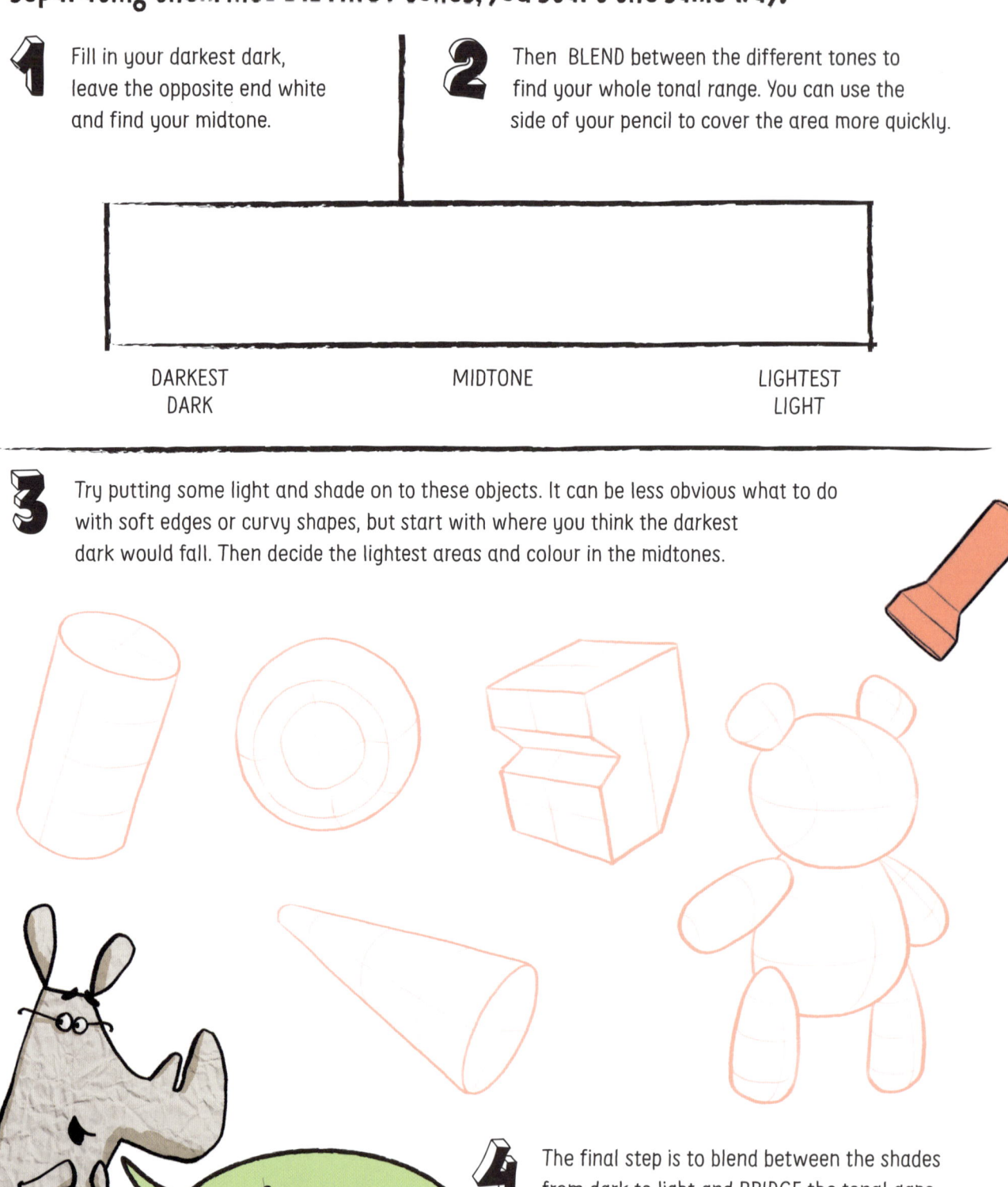

Cones, cones, cones, I could look at cones all day. Oh... I do!

4 The final step is to blend between the shades from dark to light and BRIDGE the tonal gaps. Your shapes should look amazingly 3D!

 See if you can complete this scene using everything you have learned about light, shade and tone.

Don't forget to work out which areas are darkest and lightest first.

If I eat a box of matches, will I grow up to be a dragon?

17

TOP TIP #3 Thumb Measuring

Artists often need to measure the things they are drawing to make sure that everything is in scale or has the right proportions. It's no good if the drawing of a dog is bigger than its owner (unless the owner is very far away and the dog is very close – see the next section!).

Artists invented 'thumb measuring', which is when we use one thing we can see all the time to measure something else we are looking at. It's easy!

Grab a pencil. Hold your arm out straight in front of you (don't bend at the elbow!).

Close one eye and make sure to always use the same one!

Choose a small object you can see to use as your measure. It could be a lamp in your bedroom or a car in your street.

Line up the tip of your pencil with the top of your object, and slide your thumb until it reaches the bottom of the object.

I don't think my arms are long enough!

18

Now, keeping your thumb in position and eye closed, use that measure to work out the size of other things in the scene.

How many lamps wide is your bed? Or how many cars tall is the tree on the street?

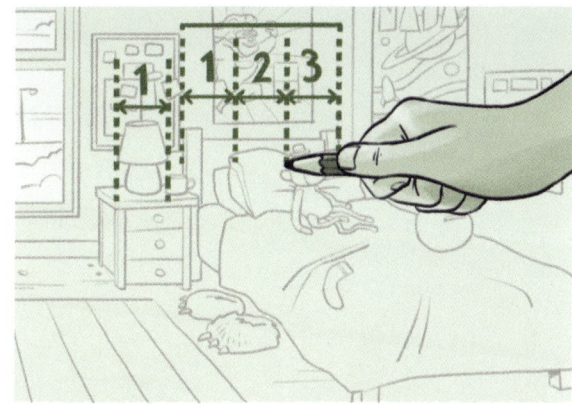

Try to sketch out the scene in front of you right now using thumb measuring to get every object in proportion, both height and width. Remember not to move from your position, otherwise the measurements will change!

BIG IDEA #2 Perspective

Things look SMALLER the further away they are from you. This is called PERSPECTIVE. To draw things in the distance, it's helpful to think about something called the VANISHING POINT on the horizon.

Imagine the horizon as a horizontal line at eye level – like the sea!

Good examples are these desert telephone poles, or these wind turbines on the ocean.

See how they appear to move further away at regular intervals while getting smaller and smaller towards a point. This is the VANISHING POINT – an imaginery point where the things you are looking at seem to disappear.

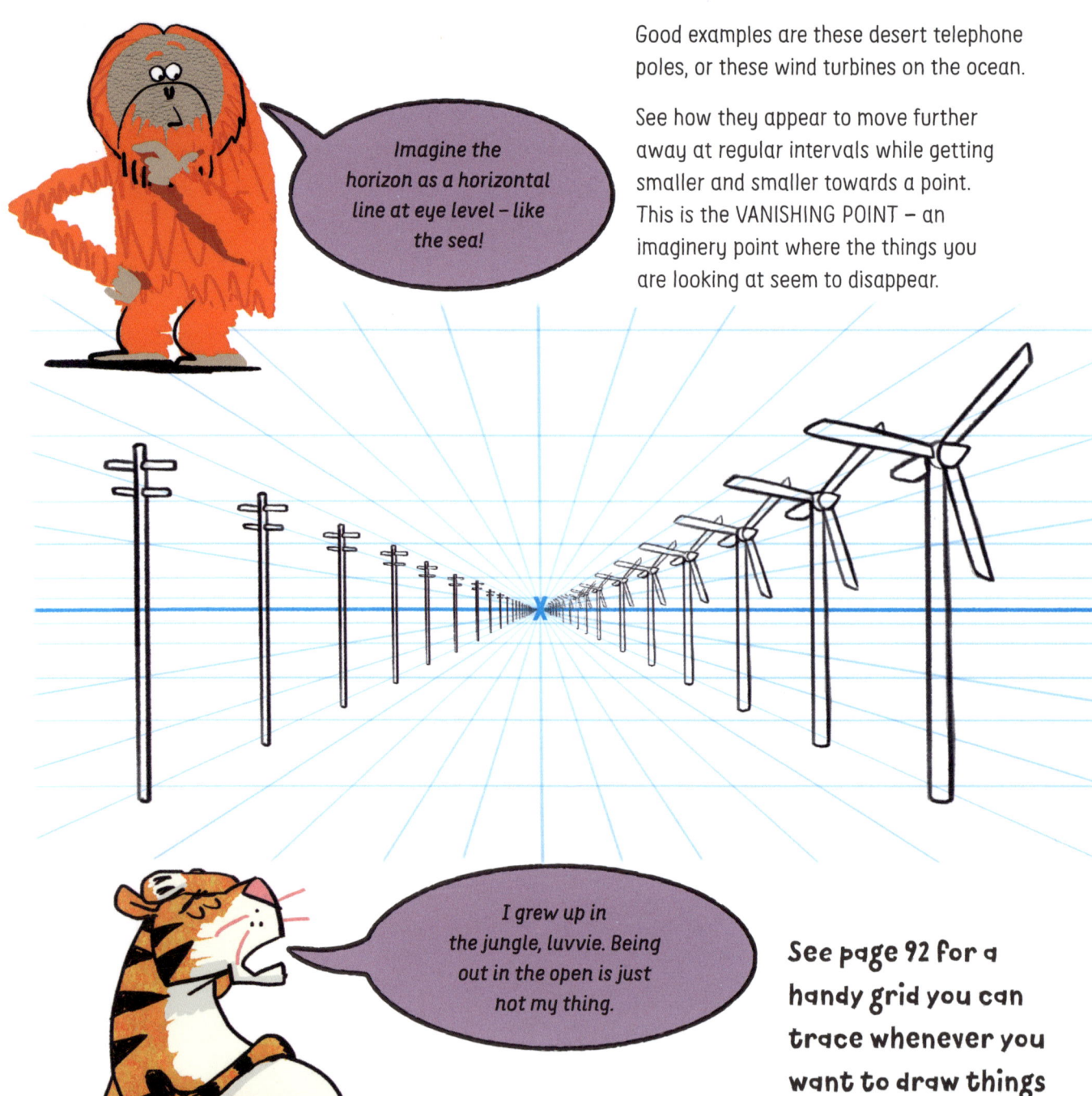

I grew up in the jungle, luvvie. Being out in the open is just not my thing.

See page 92 for a handy grid you can trace whenever you want to draw things in perspective.

20

ACTIVITY #4

 Draw some rectangles on the grid below like the ones already there. Join ALL the corners of each rectangle to the vanishing point.

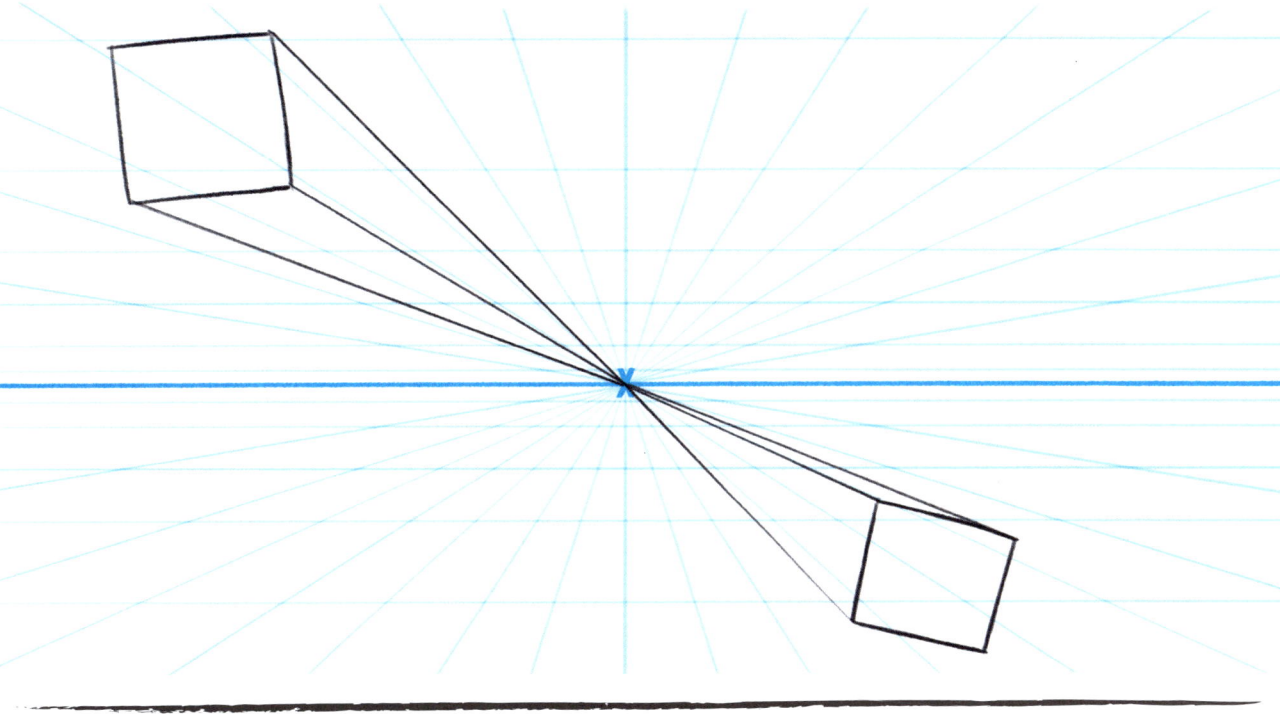

 Chop the boxes to the length you need. Now you have your boxes in perspective, you can fill them with whatever you want.

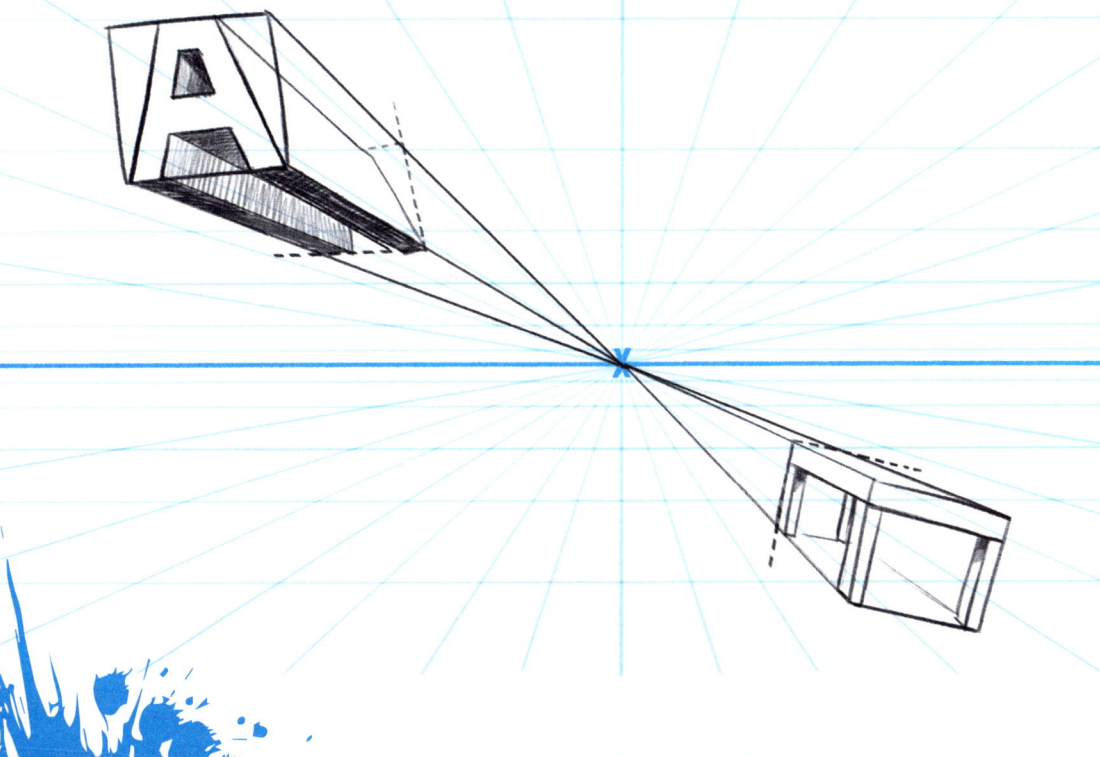

The vanishing point isn't always on the horizon (there might not be a 'horizon' in our picture, if we are indoors, or in a forest, or looking up at a building, or down into a ravine). In these cases it might be better to call it an EYELINE. Sometimes you need to IMAGINE where that eyeline is when you are drawing.

If you want something to appear ABOVE the viewer, draw it above the EYELINE.

If you want something to appear BELOW the viewer, draw it below the EYELINE.

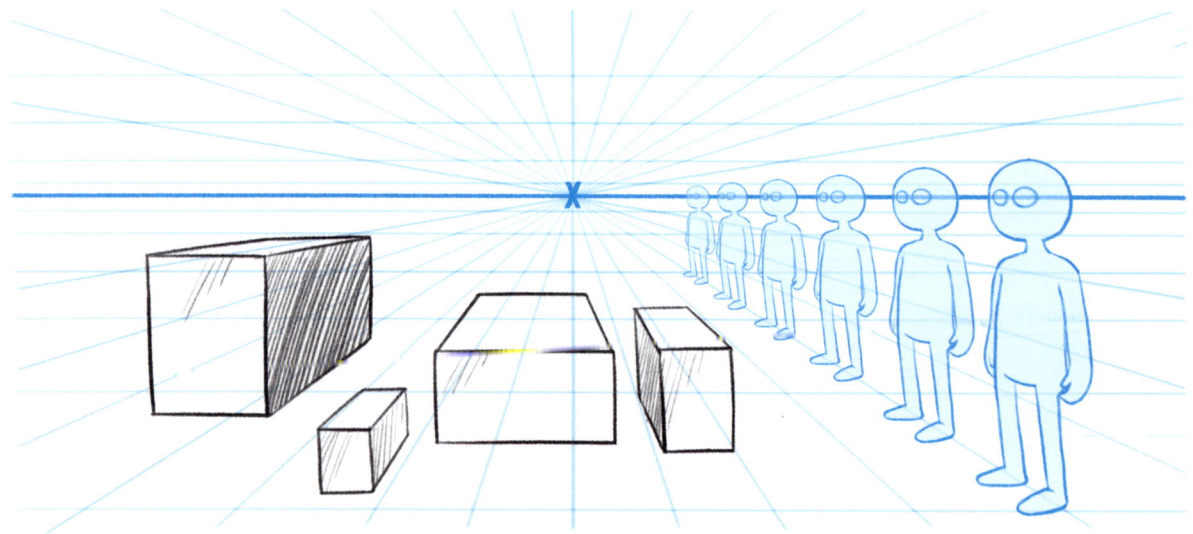

Just like with tone, it can help to block in THE EXTREMES first. Think about not only what's right in front of you in the scene, but also what's highest? What's lowest? Once you've blocked those in, you can put in the mid-high, and mid-low stuff ... then everything in between.

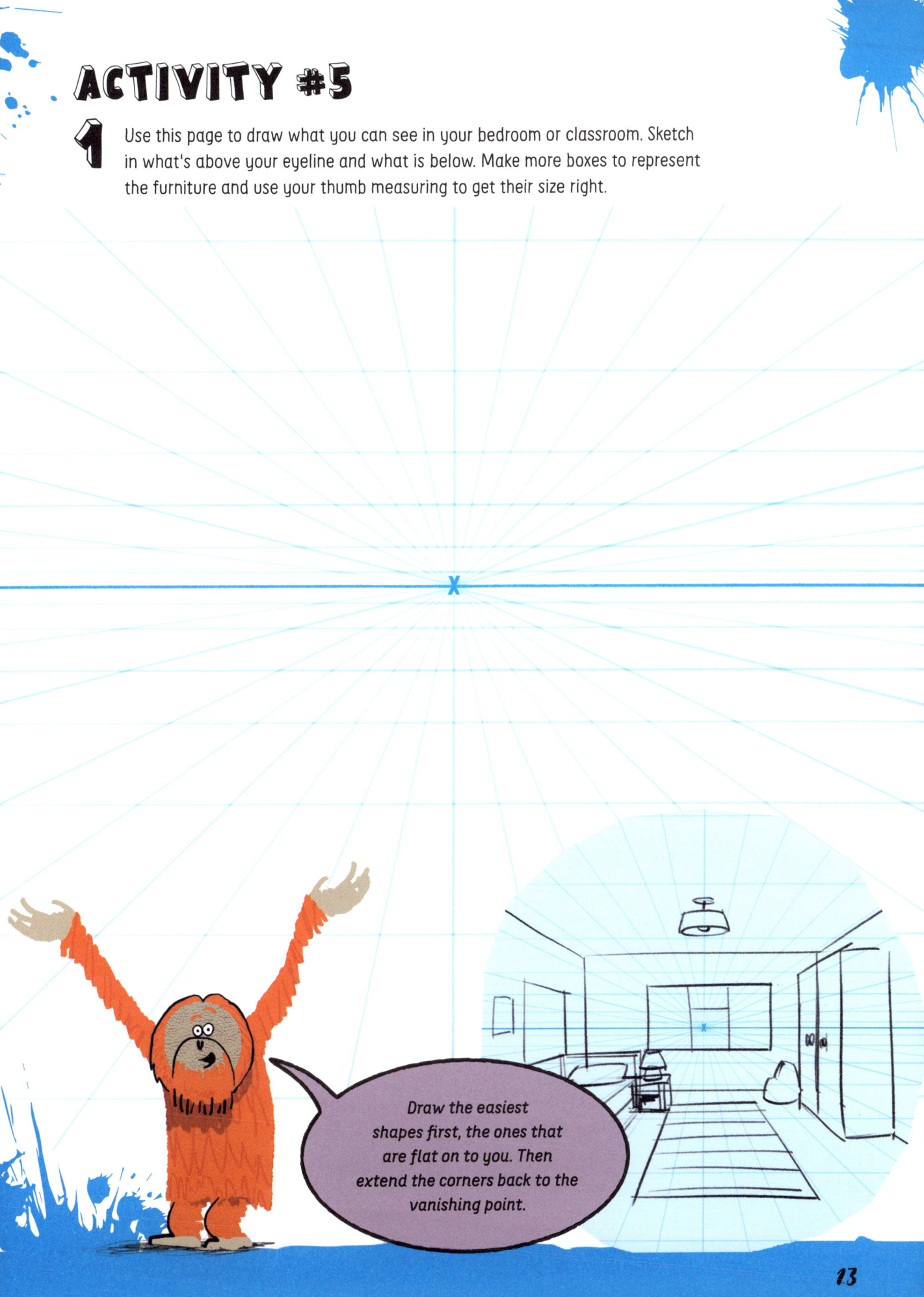

We've been using our IMAGINARY X-RAY VISION to imagine horizons and vanishing points that we can't see to draw with PERSPECTIVE. It's time to use the things we can see. Another great technique to make sure our pictures have DEPTH is to use the way objects OVERLAP each other.

These houses go back into the distance...

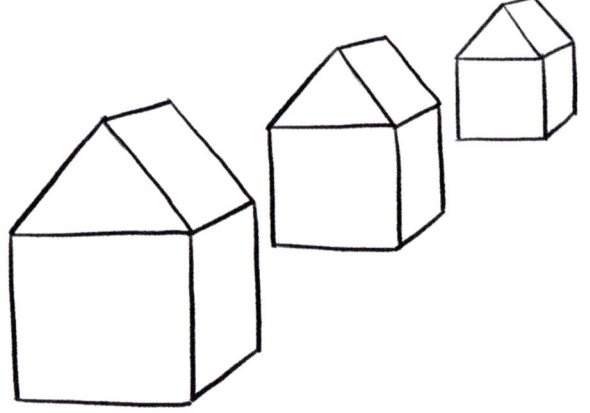

But THESE houses REALLY look as if they are one in front of the other.

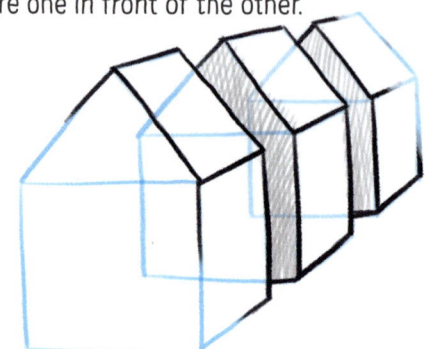

Use your light-coloured pencil to sketch in a box for each house, and then with your dark pencil, draw only the parts that would show!

It's not just separate objects that overlap each other. WHOLE THINGS OVERLAP THEMSELVES. This is called FORESHORTENING (a posh way of saying PERSPECTIVE and OVERLAP).

By using the light-coloured pencil to break this WHOLE DOG into cube parts (sorry, doggy!), you can see the separate lumps or FORMS. Next, sketch each part overlapping the other, and use the dark-coloured pencil to show only the bits you can see.

A dog chopped up into lumps? Don't mind if I do – delicious!

24

WARM-UP #1 Two-minute Triples

Try this great exercise to get you drawing.

 Set a timer for two minutes.

 You have two minutes to fill these pages with as many OBJECTS as you can. Whatever you like, but there must be THREE of each.

I promise I won't eat this page. This kind of thing tends to repeat on me.

I'm not sure I can draw three of anything!

This stops you getting bogged down staring at a blank page while making sure you focus on being concise.

BIG IDEA #3 Light, Shade and Perspective Combined, or Not...

So far, you have explored how light falls across a 3D object, but objects themselves CAST shadows. They even reflect light on to each other.

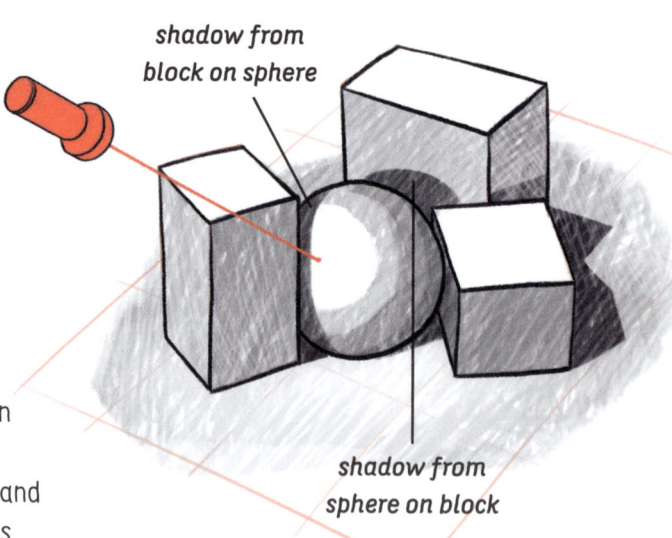

shadow from block on sphere

shadow from sphere on block

Shadows are REALLY important. They show how close objects are to each other, especially when an object overlaps another one. If you combine your overlap technique with vanishing points and light and shade, you will create very convincing 3D drawings.

Another thing to think about is that you don't always have to use the same vanishing point. Here are some 2D shapes that have been turned into 3D objects. See how the different points create different angles. You can quickly sketch to see which angle makes the shape look best.

Remember, these rules of light, shade and perspective are also things you can choose NOT to use! Sometimes it's fun just to pick one thing.

But I don't want to make things look realistic. I like cartoons... And cartoons are flat!

That's okay. Drawing in 2D doesn't mean that you can't include a sense of perspective in your pictures. By choosing to ONLY use your overlap technique, you can still create a sense of depth.

Here's a flat cartoon character. She should look NEAR and the house should appear FAR, but she just looks like a GIANT.

First, we need to move her off the horizon line. This simple change helps to 'sell' the depth of the flat shapes.

Now she overlaps the horizon.

Then add a tree that overlaps the house, but is overlapped by the girl. Adding a path to connect them helps.

Then add in your detail. What else can you add to this picture to help 'sell' the depth? A car, the sun, some clouds?

ACTIVITY #7

 Here's a scene for you to complete. This activity is about combining all three elements – overlap, tone and shadow and perspective. Work out where to put your darkest tones, your lightest tones and your midtones.

Remember, you don't always have to draw outlines. Can you make the monster look soft and furry?

WARM-UP #2 Verb-Noun Raffle

This is great fun and can result in some hilarious pictures. It's also a really good way to smash through a CREATIVE BLOCK!

 Here is a list of nouns and a list of verbs.

 Close your eyes and randomly pick one word from each list and then use these pages to draw what you've picked. For example, you could pick DOG and SNORING.

Nouns	Verbs
Cat	Baking
Crocodile	Swimming
Window	Floating
Helicopter	Sleeping
Goldfish	Breaking
Chef	Eating

Oh, I'm really not sure I'm ready for this yet. Can I have another practice?

That's what these pages are for. Don't worry, you'll get there in no time.

BIG IDEA #4 People

Drawing people can seem tricky, but if you simplify body parts into SAUSAGE, EGG, CHIPS and BEANS, you'll soon discover an easy way to create poses.

First, take a blue pencil and draw a sausage, an egg, two beans and two chips.

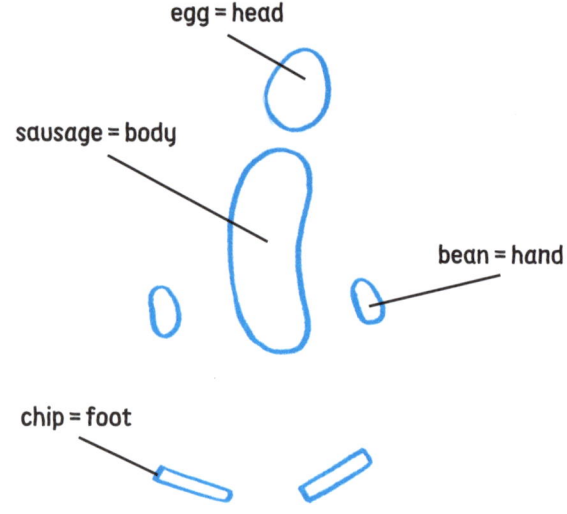

- egg = head
- sausage = body
- bean = hand
- chip = foot

Then join the shapes together with some spaghetti.

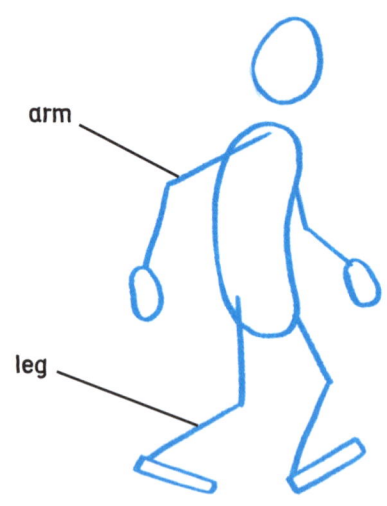

- arm
- leg

See how easy it is to create movement with some simple lines. Remember that the sausage can bend!

Now add details with a dark-coloured pencil.

34

ACTIVITY #8

 Use this page to draw lots of people moving in different ways. Are they sitting, running, or doing a cartwheel. Place the sausage, egg, chips and beans and then join them up and add detail.

Add other objects

Overlap things

Play with size and shape

We think of human bodies as 'upright', when in fact the body is similar to lots of SPRINGS stuck on top of one another. Our muscles hold us balanced, ready to SPRING or FOLD when we need to.

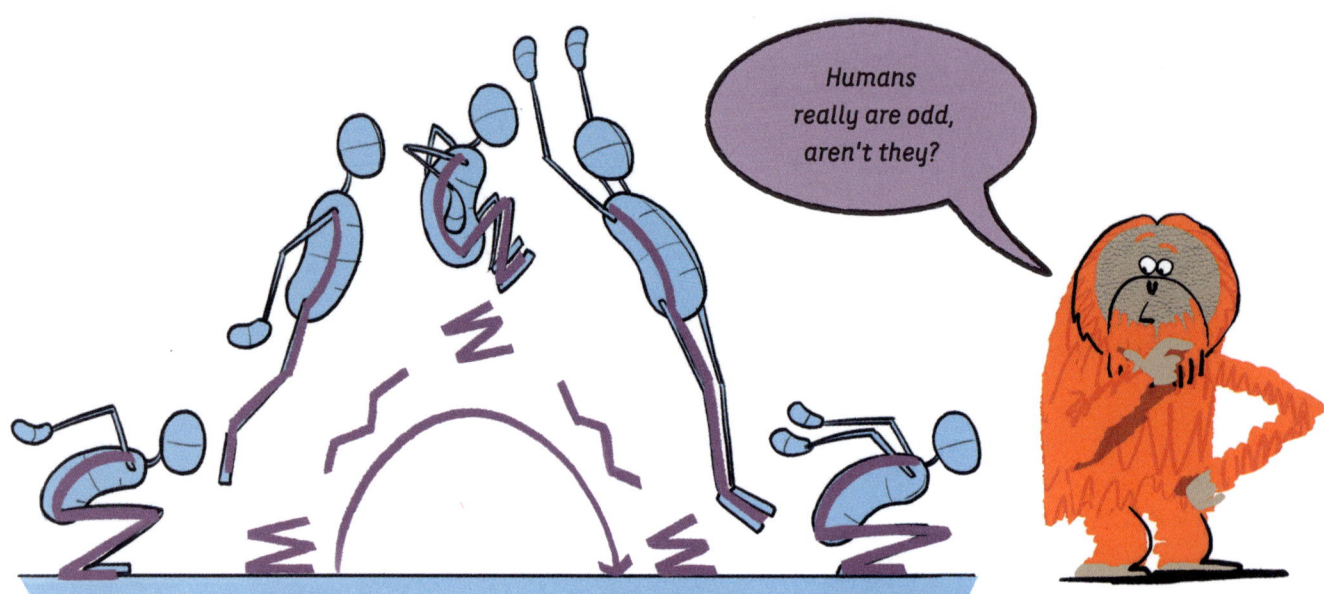

Humans really are odd, aren't they?

When standing still, people put weight on one side. Look at people in the street. Do you see anyone standing like a soldier at attention? It's natural to lean to one side or the other as it's more comfortable and uses less muscle energy.

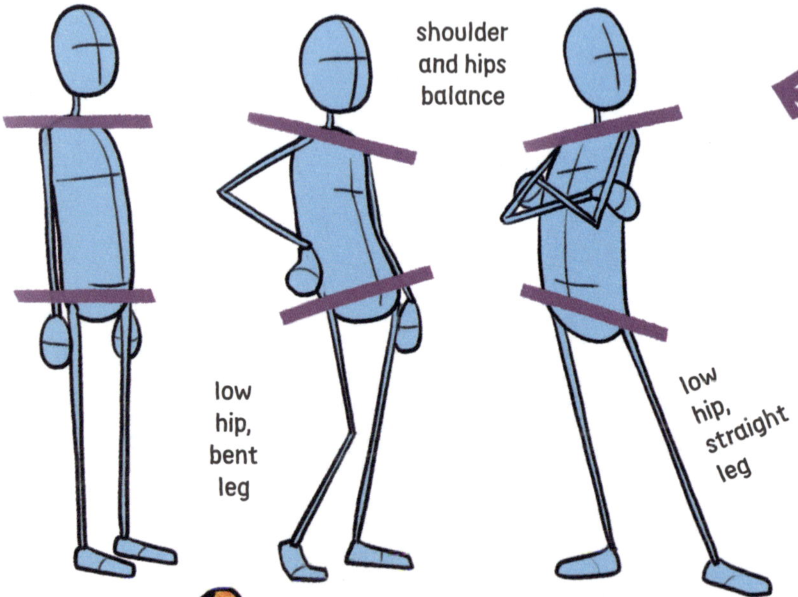

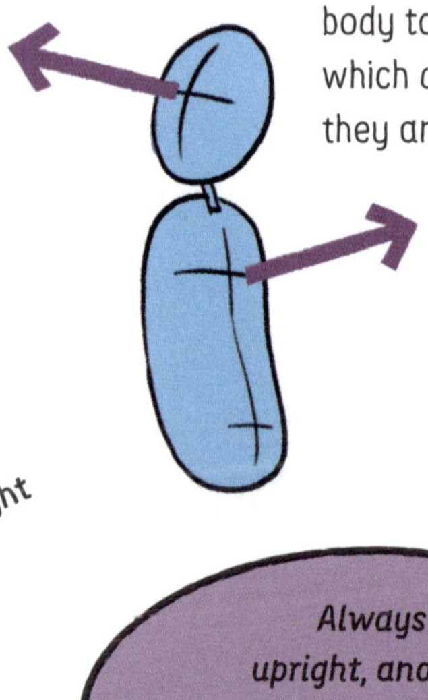

shoulder and hips balance

Use the cross on the face or body to show which direction they are facing.

low hip, bent leg

low hip, straight leg

Always upright, and not a jot of camouflage... And they say I'm a show-off!

36

ACTIVITY #9

1 Use this page to draw people you can see standing or sitting still – ask your friends or family if they will pose for you. Do they have their own way of standing or sitting? Notice how they balance their weight. Is it to one side or the other?

2 Use your sausage, eggs, chips and beans to quickly sketch the pose and then add in detail. Don't worry about the face – that's BIG IDEA #5!

Posture can show energy. High or low energy can indicate emotion.

Body posture can tell a story.

37

Let's try drawing some action poses. One way to think about action is that the body is FALLING. If you combine that with how the body BALANCES itself, you will be able to draw really convincing poses.

Use a vertical line through your pose to check the BALANCE.

Static poses have all the weight centred around the vertical line.

In this pose, the body is further away from the centre line and is falling on to the front foot.

Here, the head and body are completely off centre so the arms and other leg are thrown out forwards to try to regain balance.

POSTURE is a very good way to convey expression. Look at the difference between the two poses below. The body is in a seated position, but in the first illustration, the figure looks tired and dejected. In the second, the figure is alert and positive.

I'm really good at expressing myself as a log... Does that count?

ACTIVITY #10

1 Use this page to draw different action poses! Try drawing someone dancing or playing football. The key is to start fast and draw in the line of action. Then you can wrap the body shape around that line. Capture the feeling and the energy!

TOP TIP #4 Use a shadow underneath your character to show the ground... Just a smear or a sketched line will help 'sell' where the character is touching the ground (or not).

We express ourselves with our WHOLE bodies, but we ACTIVELY express with our hands as much as we do with our faces. A hand can seem tricky at first, so let's break it down into small steps.

Think of the hand as a MITTEN. The palm, the thumb sticking out and the fingers all as one 'flap' coming from the palm.

See how the thumb FOLDs the palm in half sometimes.

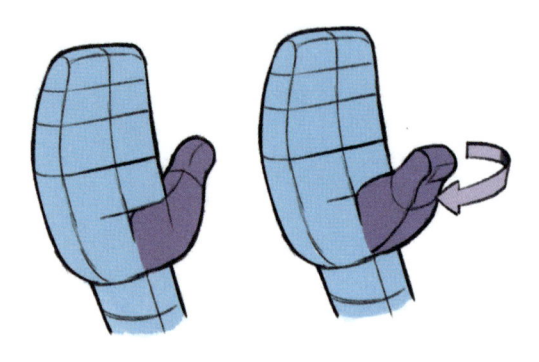

The fingers 'follow' each other, either spread wide or together.

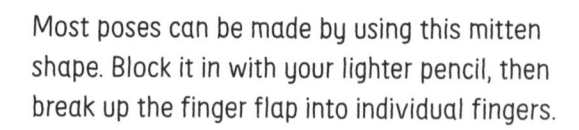

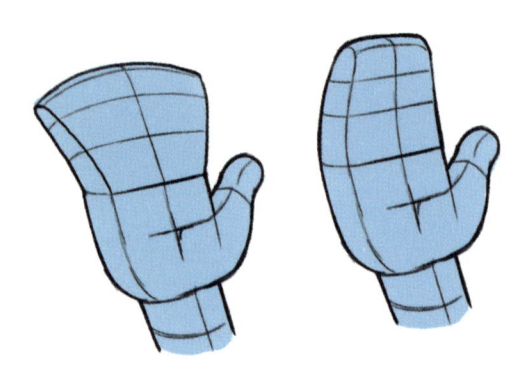

Most poses can be made by using this mitten shape. Block it in with your lighter pencil, then break up the finger flap into individual fingers.

Wow... I always thought they were just cocktail sausages for starters.

TOP TIP #5

The middle and ring finger normally follow each other closely. Some old cartoon characters even have these MERGED into the same finger!

ACTIVITY #11

1 Here are some expressive MITTENS. Break them up and draw in the fingers.

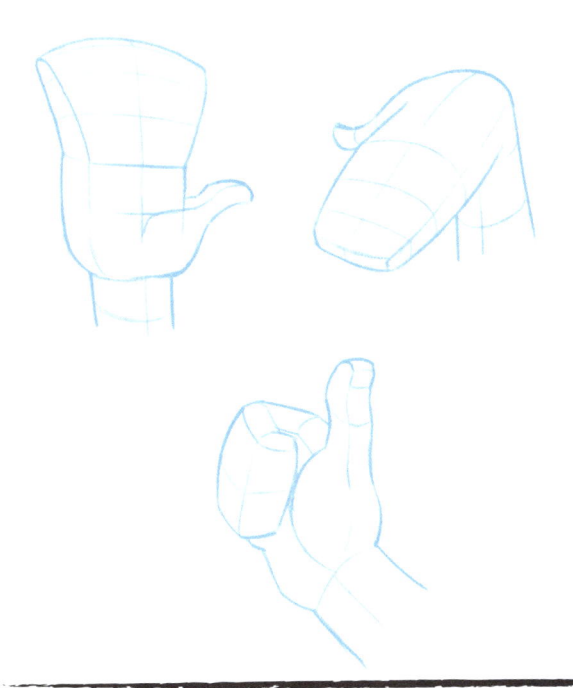

2 These hand poses have fingers that DON'T follow each other. Trace over them then draw two more.

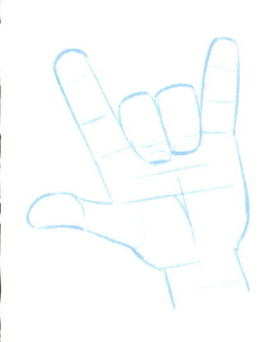

3 Now look at these characters. Can you draw their hand positions to match the body pose? It's up to you! Act out the emotion and see what your hand does.

41

WARM-UP #3 Blind Drawing

Tie a scarf round your head to make sure you can't see anything!

1 Choose an item from the list below. Then close your eyes and see how well you can draw it without looking.

Choose from this list!
- Cat
- Dog
- Space rocket
- Bicycle
- Ice cream
- Pineapple

Now we're talking! Squiggle-tastic!

The idea is to try to do an accurate drawing.

I think I might be able to manage this one.

This is to train you to trust your hand, and to FEEL where it is going rather than SEEING it.

BIG IDEA #5 Human Faces

Humans are WIRED to look for faces from birth. You see them everywhere, so they're often what you end up drawing the most. Let's learn how to draw EXPRESSIVE faces – how to show someone looking happy, sad, angry or even VILLAINOUS!

Most heads have similar proportions. Here are some of the basic rules to remember when drawing faces.

Not all of us! Some of us have very different proportions!

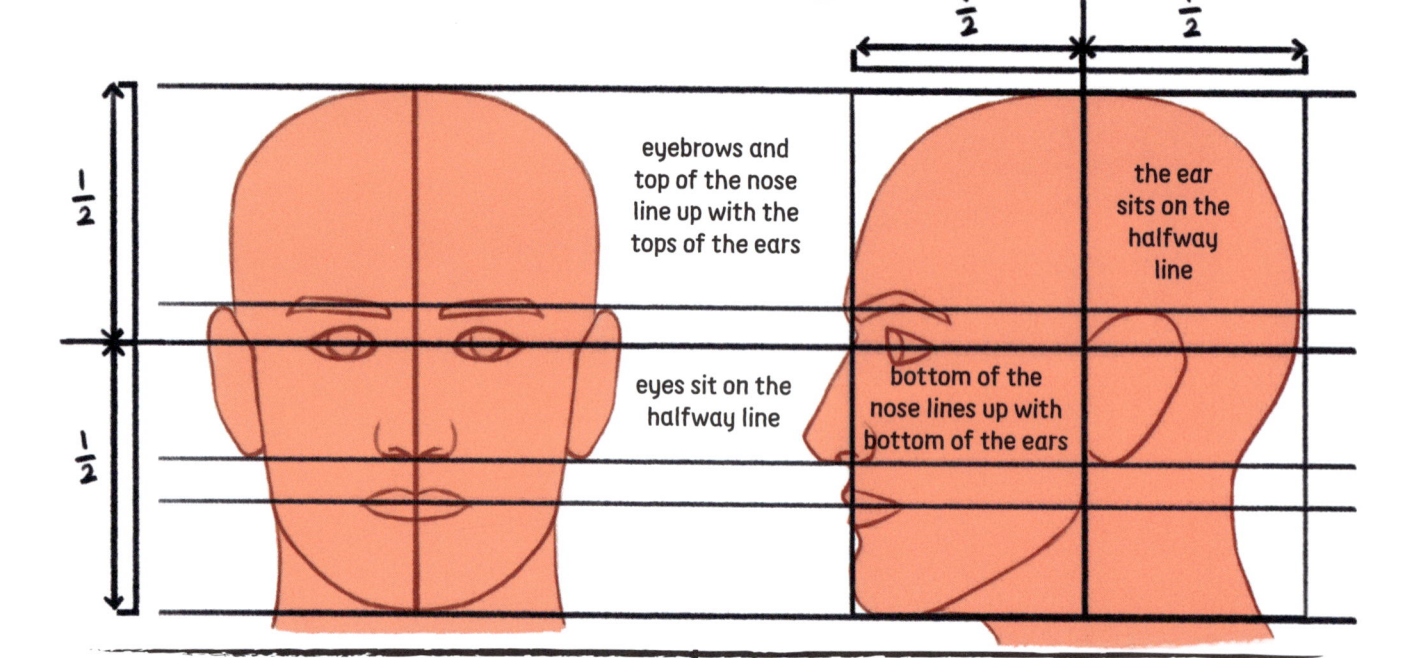

eyebrows and top of the nose line up with the tops of the ears

the ear sits on the halfway line

eyes sit on the halfway line

bottom of the nose lines up with bottom of the ears

To show movement in the head and face, you need to break the head down into simpler CHUNKS THAT MOVE. Think of the skull like a loaf of bread that is sitting on top of a broom handle – or neck.

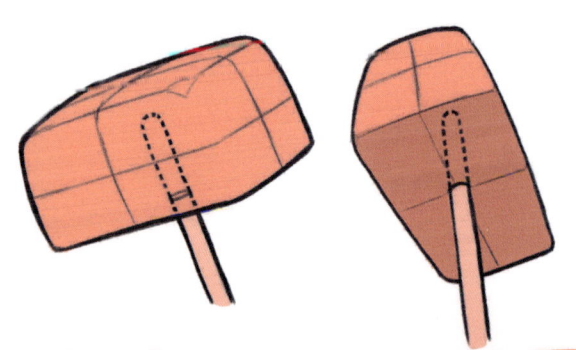

Then add half a loaf for the mouth and chin. The jawbone hinges from your ear.

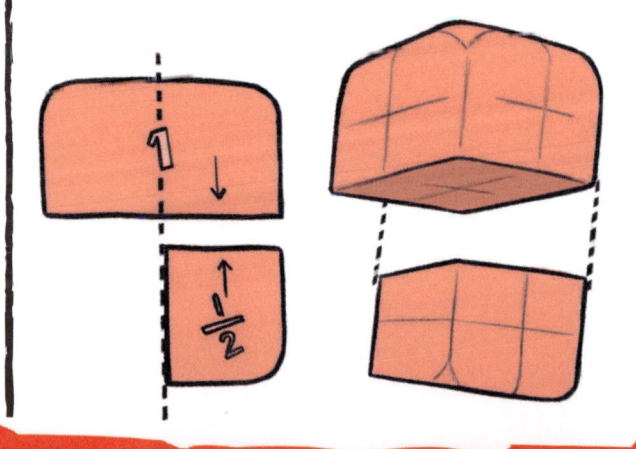

44

Next, add the prominent features. The eyes go where the loaves join, on the same line as the ears. The nose is a triangular wedge for now.

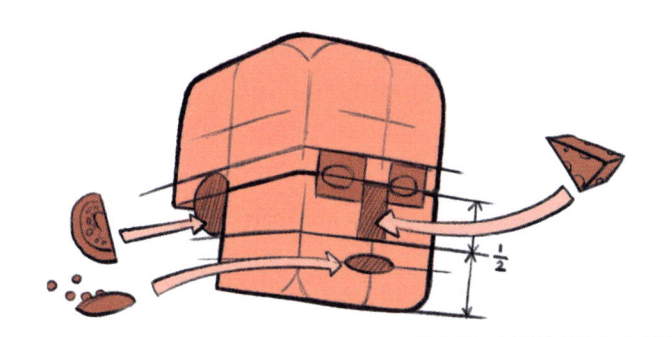

Then round off the corners and adjust.

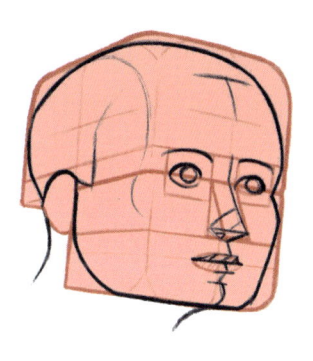

ACTIVITY #12

1 Draw different heads over these 'loaf-heads'. Choose someone you know well or find a picture to copy. How do their features map on to the loaf?

Alas, poor Yorick... I ate him well.

45

Eyes are considered to be the 'window to someone's soul'! Creating expression in the eyes is really easy and will make your characters come to life.

Start by simplifying the eye down to LASH LINES and EYE BLOB.

The main thing you 'read' is the shape made by the lash lines that cover the pupil or eye blob.

Now you can add eyebrows and creases to create character and expression!

This works with lots of different styles. Try a few and have fun finding your own eye style!

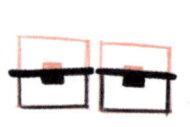

Don't draw until you see the whites of their eyes!

46

Where eyes LOOK can add even more expression.

Closed eyes can still send a message.

Both eyes don't have to match, either!

ACTIVITY #13

Use the figures below to practise your eye expressions. What expression do you think goes with the pose? Is there more than one answer?

Pupil comes from 'pupilla', meaning little doll in Latin, because we see a 'little doll' of ourselves in others' eyes.

47

Just like the eyes, humans are brilliant at reading mouth shapes for communication, but it can sometimes be difficult to capture the right expression when drawing. Don't worry, here are some tips to simplify things.

Simplify the mouth to where the lips meet the teeth (liplines), teeth and a hole.

Look at the shapes made by contrasting areas. Top teeth against the dark inside of the mouth, or bottom teeth.

The mouth muscles and jaw create folds and dimples in the whole face as they move. These amplify the expression.

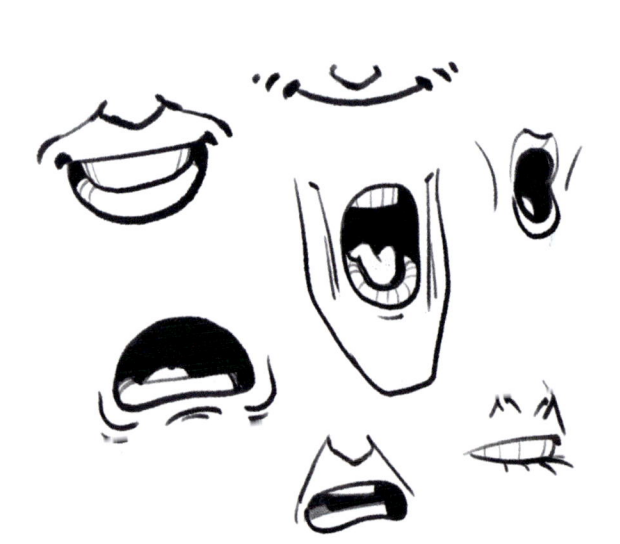

Experiment with different styles, but how you read expression will stay the same.

I think I have two emotions. Hungry and very hungry.

48

Asymetry is good. Both sides of the face don't need to look the same.

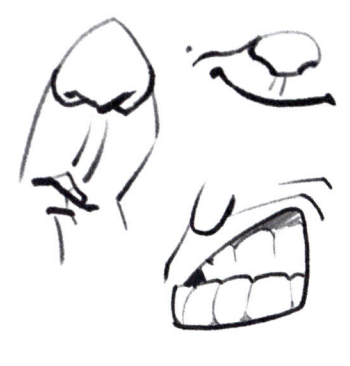

The mouth is three-dimensional. The lips wrap around the teeth and stretch up and back.

Gums, lips, moustaches all add character, but the rules stay the same.

ACTIVITY #14

1 Draw your own mouth expression on the heads below. How does it change with the mouth open or closed?

Don't forget to look in your mirror to see how your mouth moves!

49

Now you know how to draw expressive eyes and mouths individually, but you judge someone's expression through their EYES and MOUTH combined.

This combination can amplify each other – if both the eyes and mouth show the same feeling – for bolder emotions such as JOY, RAGE or SADNESS.

Or the two elements can contradict each other, to express a more subtle emotion, such as being NERVOUS or UNCERTAIN.

Usually the EYES show the real emotion.

Rhinos express themselves with their horns!

50

ACTIVITY #15

1 It's your turn! Try combining what you've learned about eye and mouth expressions to create different emotions on these faces. Then draw your own!

Watch your nostrils as you pull a mouth shape. They can amplify the expression too!

51

TOP TIP #6 Line-edge Quality

The soft or hard edges between areas of tone can show how harshly or softly things are LIT, but edges can also show what type of material something is made from.

This fluffy, furry outline is defined by broken lines and light, feathery strokes

A crisp edge here shows shine

Crisp, smooth edges indicate smooth and shiny metal

Broken varied dancing lines and edges imply motion and energy

Lines can also add personality to the thing you are drawing. What do these lines look like they are FEELING? Calm? Excited? What would you draw with each line type? Experiment in this space using each line type or invent one of your own!

51

Just remember that anything looks better with stripes.

BIG IDEA #6 Animals

If you can draw people, you can draw animals. Yes, they do have extra legs, which might be different lengths, but they still bend in the same way as humans.

Let's take a closer look at sausage person's skeleton. The torso is made up of a ribcage and a pelvis, joined by a spine.

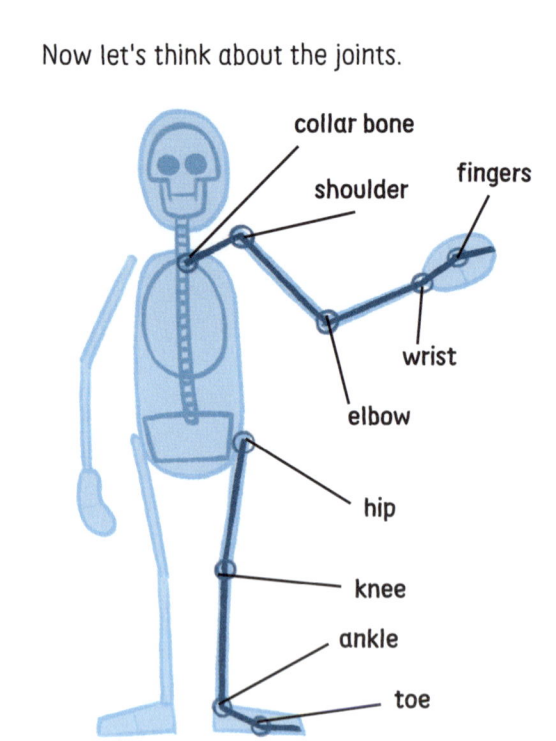

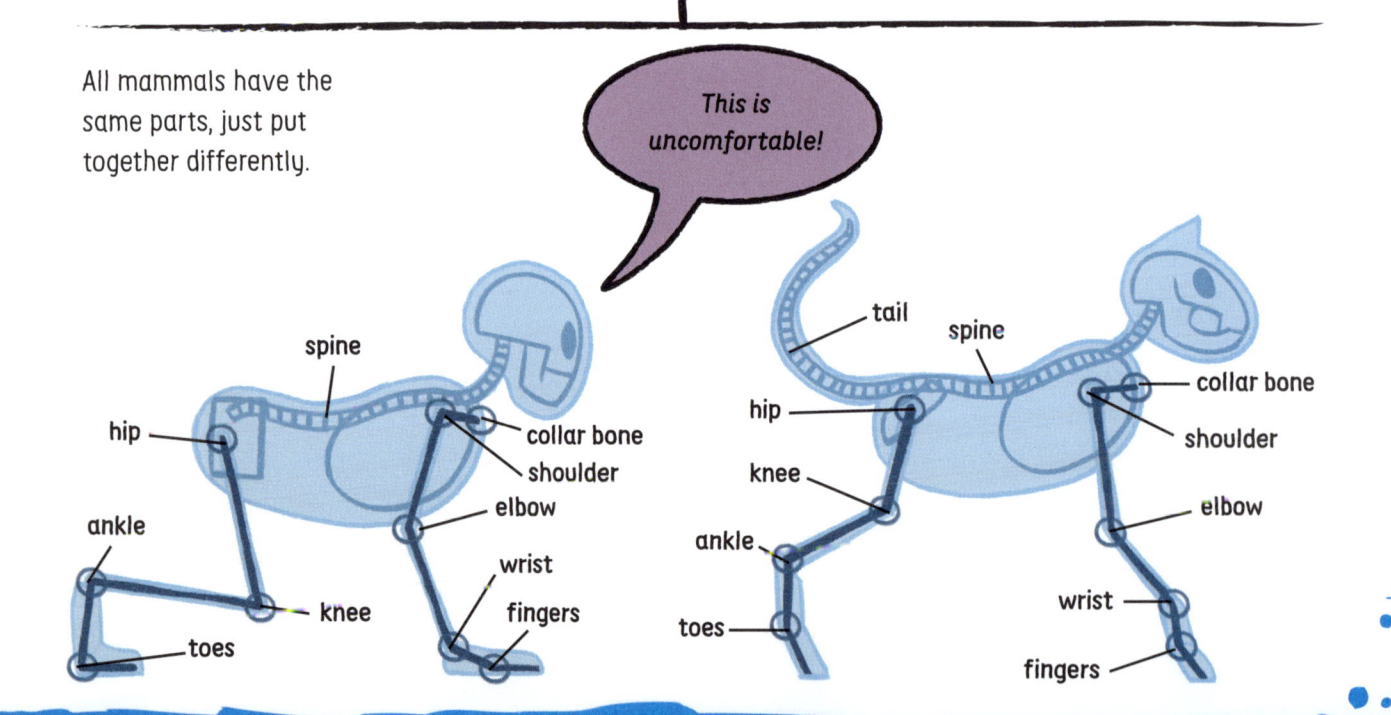

Now let's think about the joints.

- collar bone
- shoulder
- fingers
- wrist
- elbow
- hip
- knee
- ankle
- toe

All mammals have the same parts, just put together differently.

This is uncomfortable!

- spine
- hip
- ankle
- toes
- knee
- collar bone
- shoulder
- elbow
- wrist
- fingers

- tail
- spine
- hip
- knee
- ankle
- toes
- collar bone
- shoulder
- elbow
- wrist
- fingers

ACTIVITY #16

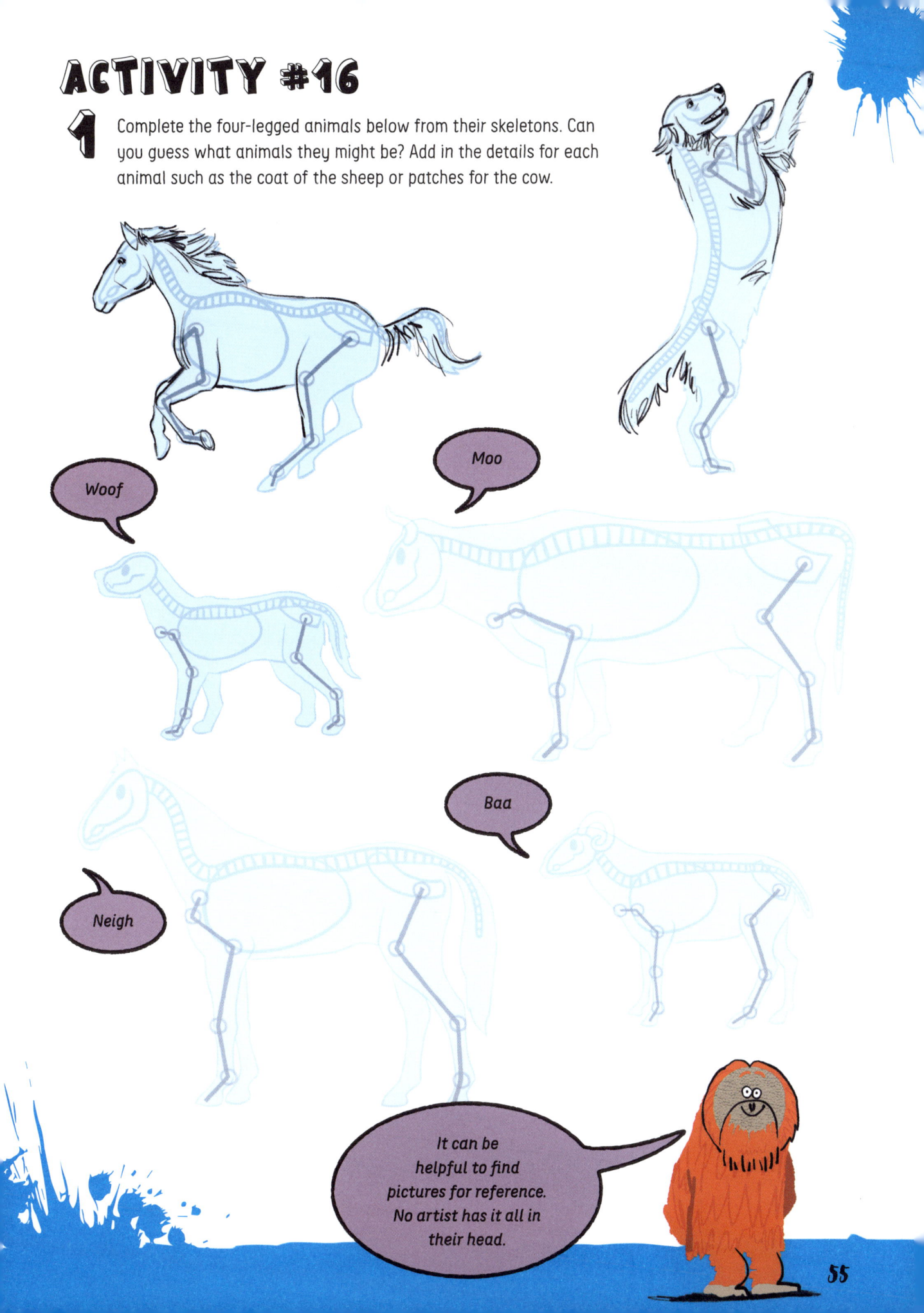

1 Complete the four-legged animals below from their skeletons. Can you guess what animals they might be? Add in the details for each animal such as the coat of the sheep or patches for the cow.

Woof

Moo

Baa

Neigh

It can be helpful to find pictures for reference. No artist has it all in their head.

When drawing animals, anything with a SPINE will follow most of the same rules as the four-legged mammals on the previous page.

A chimpanzee is similar to a human. It just has different bone lengths and joint rotations. A frog, and even a fish, share similarities. They all have a skull, a jaw, a spine and limbs.

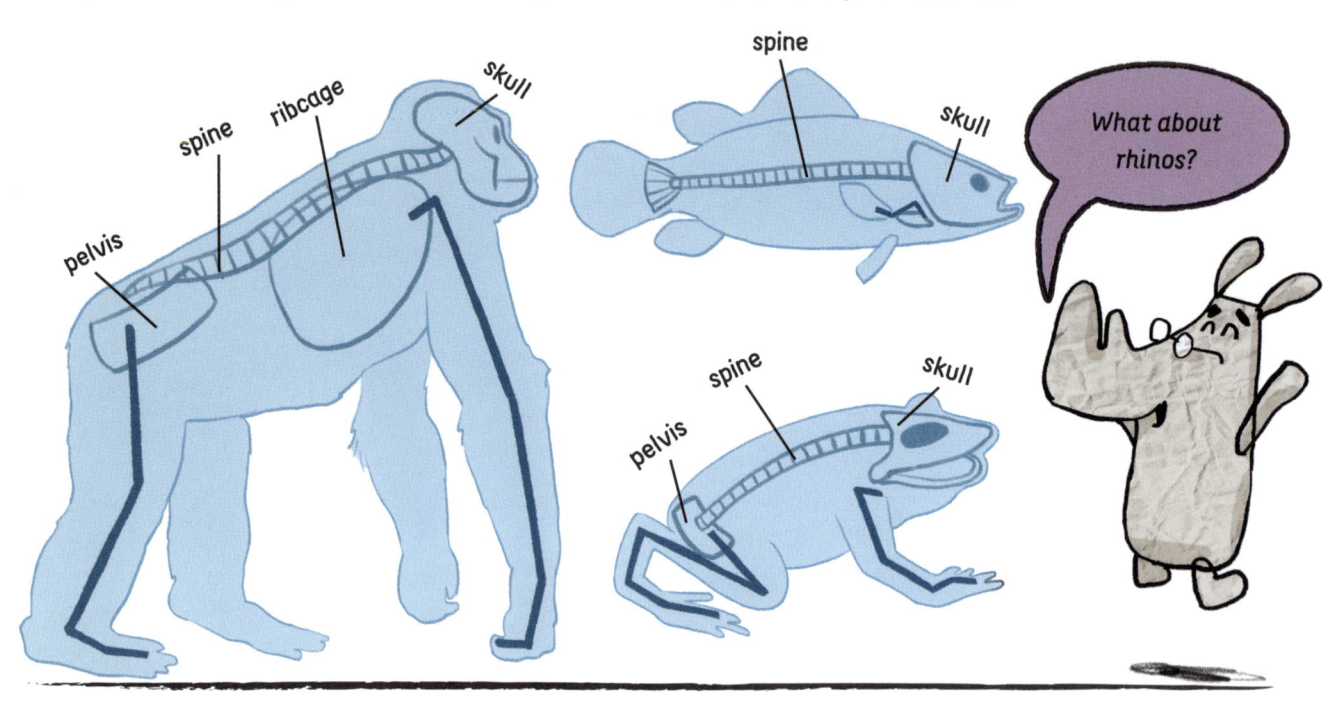

What about rhinos?

What about creatures that are EXTINCT, or fantasy creatures? Find a starting point and go from there. For instance, there are lots of similarities between a T-Rex and a chicken.

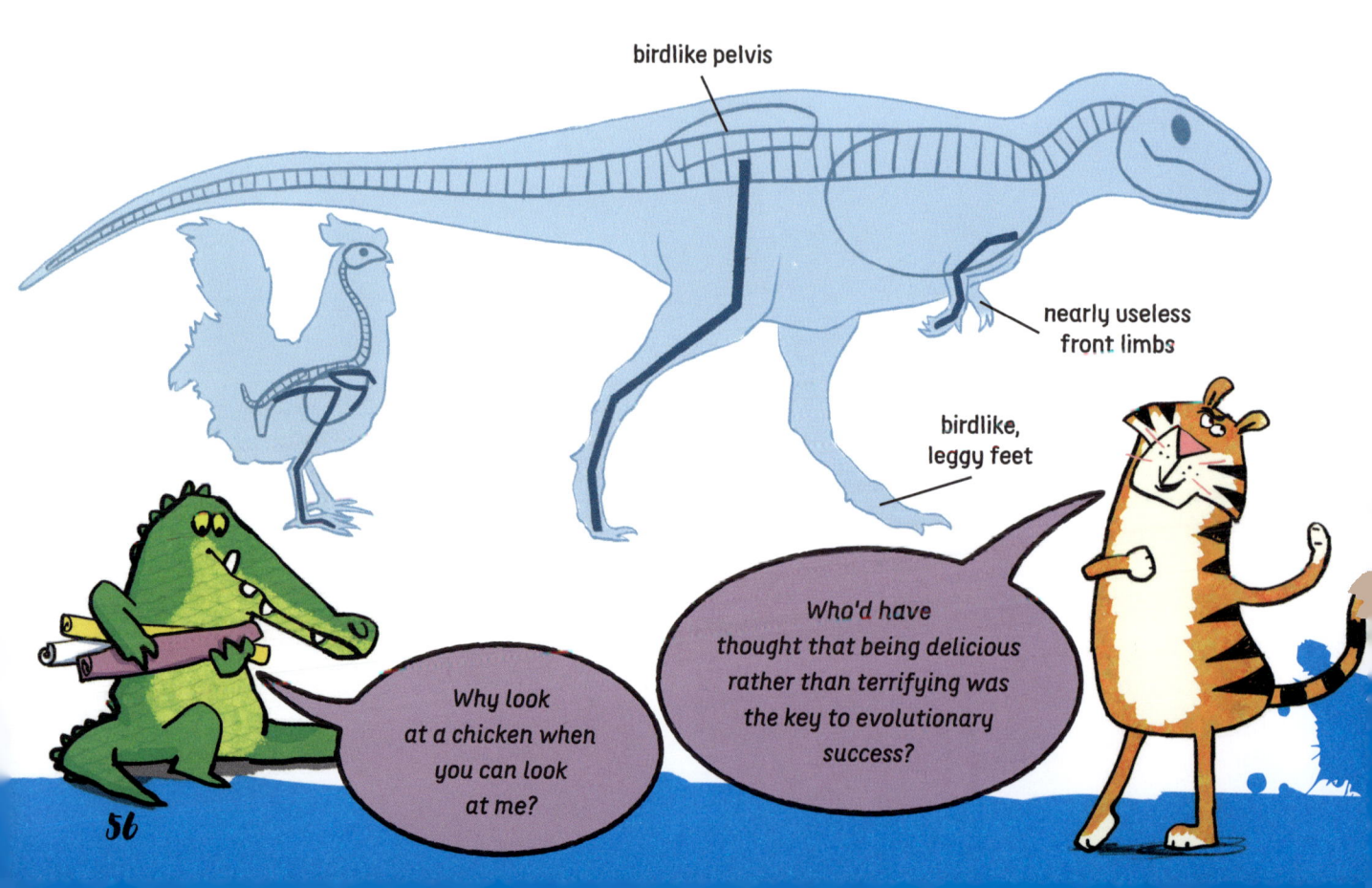

Why look at a chicken when you can look at me?

Who'd have thought that being delicious rather than terrifying was the key to evolutionary success?

ACTIVITY #17

1 How many fantasy creatures can you create? Which animals are they based on? Finish off the sketches below or draw your own on the blank pages at the end of the book.

57

Although insects and other creatures such as jellyfish are VERY different to mammals, they can also be broken down in the same way. Think about the CORE SHAPES first and then add in detail.

Many insects are made up of three key parts.

head　thorax　abdomen

They have their skeleton on the outside, but it's still really FLEXIBLE. The plates slide over each other. They're like tiny little machines. Great inspiration for making up robots!

Ugh, that looks like the sort of things I pick out of my teeth.

Creatures from under the sea are built for a very different environment. A fabulous starting point for ALIENS FROM SPACE or even SPACESHIPS!

58

ACTIVITY #18

1 Try drawing your own insects or sea creatures. What similarities are there between vertebrates (animals with spines) and invertebrates (animals without spines)?

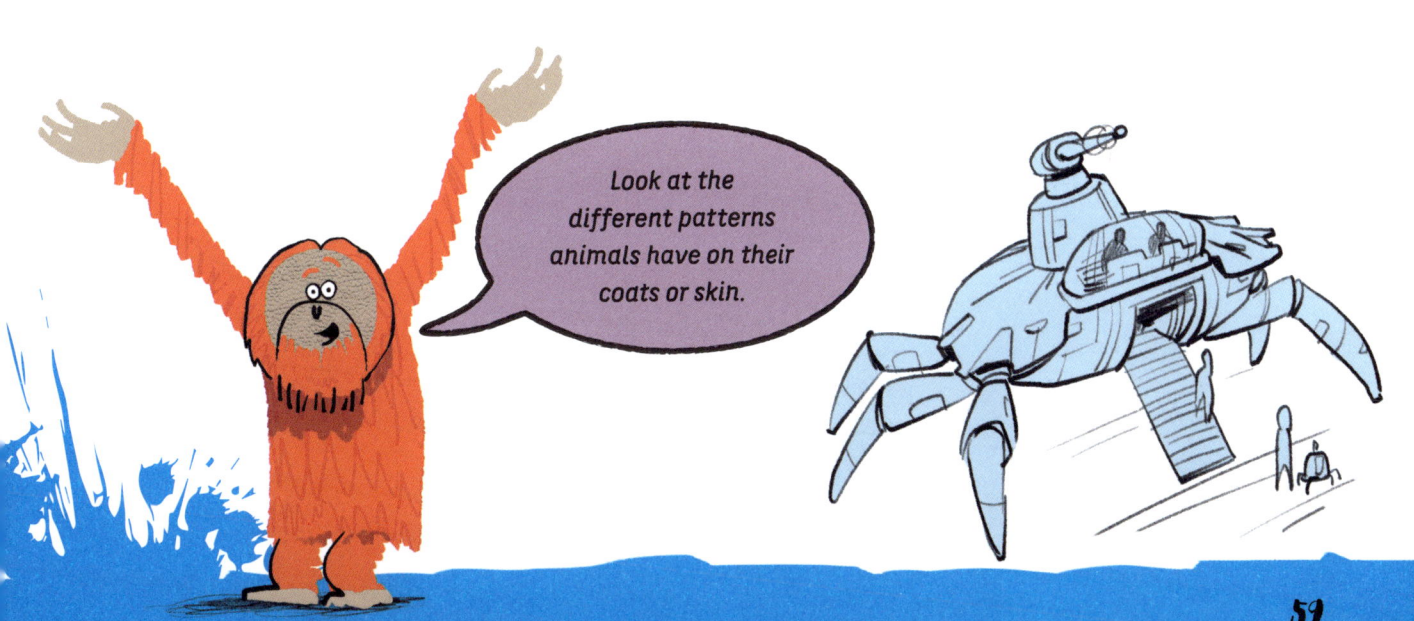

Look at the different patterns animals have on their coats or skin.

WARM-UP #4 One-line Drawing

Simply ... don't lift the pencil off the paper when you're drawing. Choose something you can see in front of you and try to draw it with only one line. Use these blank pages to have a go!

YYYYYAAAAAAAAAYY!
Squiggly squoggly again!

> I think I'm starting to get this. Lino-rhino, that's what they call me!

BIG IDEA #7 Vehicles

You've learned how to draw a lot of ORGANIC things, but how about some man-made objects? Let's start with a CAR.

A car is basically two boxes. One for sitting in and one for holding the engine. The wheels go somewhere BALANCED.

Let's draw it from the front and the side. Use simple shapes to create the details.

Apply what you learned about perspective to transfer that shape to a 3D box.

Sketch with your light-coloured pencil, shaving off and adding bits to the overall shape until you're happy. Finish with your dark-coloured pencil.

May I suggest adding 'go-faster' stripes?

ACTIVITY #19

1 Use this space to draw your own car. You can play with the design as you might play with a character. Add spoilers, exhaust pipes, cracks or scratches. Think about who might own it. Draw some whizzy lines underneath to make it look as if it's moving, or even FLYING off the ground.

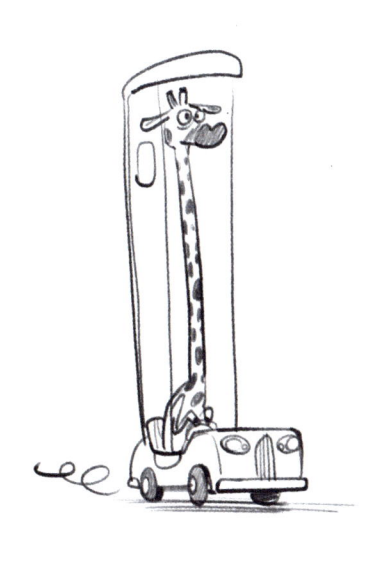

Vehicles, usually metal, are often shiny. Use your line-edge quality skills to add shine.

You can build up other vehicles in the same way. Work out your ideas in 2D – front and side views – and then sketch out a cube of two and move your design over into 3D.

ACTIVITY #20

1 Let's design a monster truck! Start with the front and side views. How many headlights does it have? Does it have decal stickers or roof lights? What about the exhaust pipe? Add your ideas to the outline below.

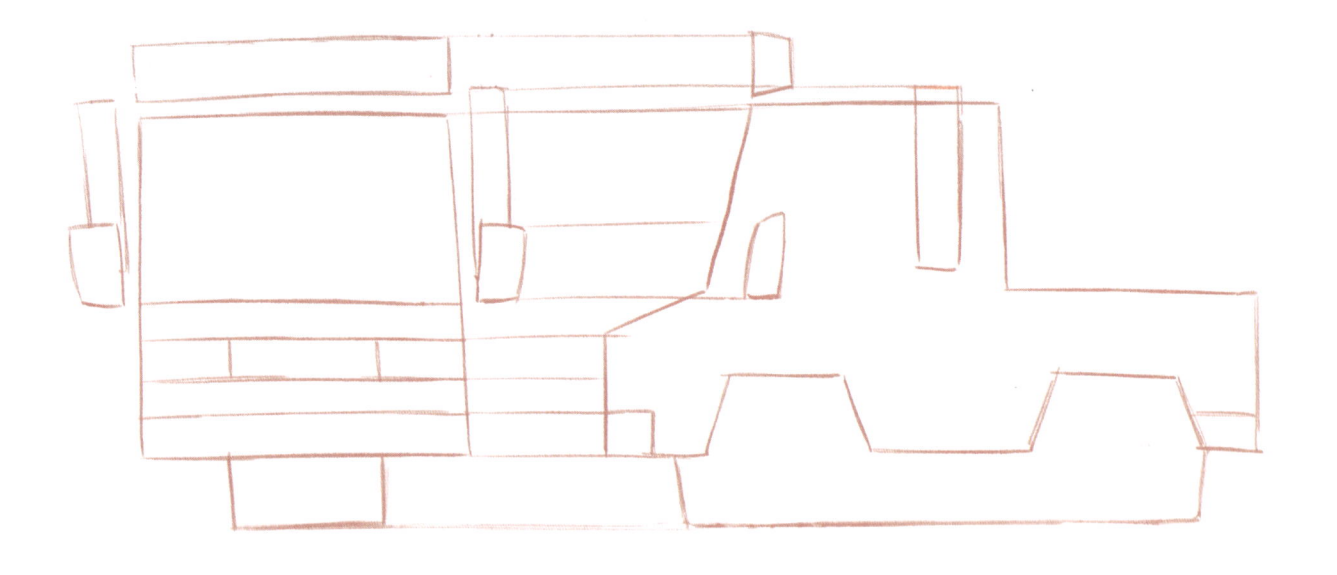

2 Move those ideas over to a 3D perspective. Use your light-coloured pencil to sketch in the shapes you want and add the detail with your dark--coloured pencil.

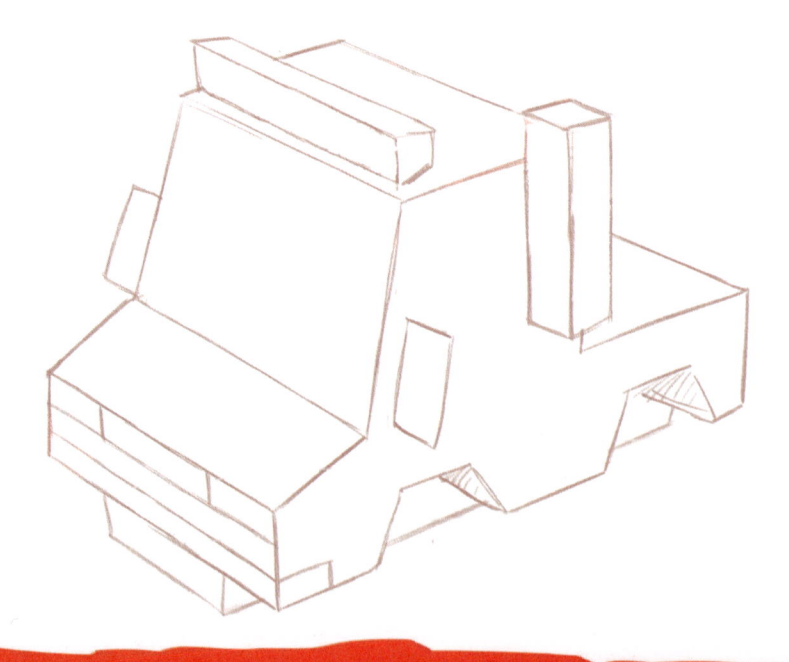

3 Now let's try an action sequence. Add your final design to this dynamic view. What is your truck jumping over?

I always get in trouble for beeping my horn!

WARM-UP #5 Quick Draw

This exercise times you drawing the same thing. Choose an item from the list below, then draw it three times. Each time taking MORE time than the previous attempt. What has happened to your drawing by the end of the activity?

30 Seconds

Choose from this list!
- Burger
- Skyscraper
- Squirrel
- Dolphin
- Alien
- Teddy

Oh yeah! I can feel a scribble coming on.

1 Minute

3 Minutes

Remember, quick doesn't necessarily mean messy. Why don't you try to use as few lines as possible?

BIG IDEA #8 Buildings

You might think buildings are too difficult to draw, because they're SO BIG. The trick is to realise that you don't have to draw every brick or every roof tile, in the same way that you didn't need to draw every eyelash on a face.

The first thing to do is to take your light-coloured pencil and draw the BIG outline of your building.

It's a good idea to give the building some scale, so including a tiny human really helps.

Now you know how tall the building is, you can add doors at the right height.

If you'd be so kind as to design me a palace, please... Something like the Taj Mahal will do nicely!

Next let's sketch in a grid. This will help you to add in windows, or drainpipes.

You can HINT at brick, or wooden planks by sketching in sections. Your brain will fill in the rest!

Once you've worked out your ideas in 2D, you could even sketch out a cube and apply the same rules in 3D!

My cousin has a lovely place in New York. The nicest sewer you ever saw!

Buildings have character too. The kind of material a building is made from will affect its shape and indicate what type of building it might be.

Modern buildings made of concrete, steel and brick are usually taller, with clean edges.

Older buildings made of heavier materials are lower and have fewer straight edges.

Use your vertical line with buildings too. Most buildings need to sit squarely on the CENTRE OF GRAVITY line, otherwise your eye perceives them to be falling over.

Use this to your advantage to create a FANTASY BUILDING that breaks these rules.

Most of my buildings tend to lean too.

70

ACTIVITY #21

1 Here are some building shapes for you to work with. Try adding a human for scale, and then add in the details. Think about what the buildings are used for. Are they nice places to live, or is one scary?

Use the pages at the back of the book to sketch an entire city by adding blocks together.

WARM-UP #6 Scribble Monsters

This is fun to do on your own, or play with a friend. Using your light-coloured pencil, start by squiggling a random shape. Then take your dark-coloured pencil and make sense of the squiggle. Perhaps it will become a face, a figure, an animal, a landscape or a monster?

Play with friends by swapping over after you've squiggled!

BIG IDEA #9 Nature

Nature is a huge subject but let's start by learning how to draw one of the most common things found in the natural world – a tree.

Once again, its all about the BIG IDEA. Consider a tree.

You don't need to draw every single branch or leaf. SQUINT at it through your eyelashes and find the BIG SHAPES. The trunk, an outline of where the leaves reach and any gaps.

Look at the direction of the big branches

Draw in the detail of the branches and trunk, then use the side of your pencil to block in the foliage.

Fill in leaf details with dark squiggles, or use your eraser to add highlights by taking away the pencil shading.

Look for overlap. Trees are 3D and twisty!

74

ACTIVITY #22

1 Now it's your turn. Find a tree in your garden or a park, or even a picture of one online. Follow the steps on the previous page and see what you can draw.

Remember, it's your job to decide what to show and what not to show.

ACTIVITY #23

Now let's use the same principles to draw other objects from nature such as flowers, plants, shells and rocks.

1 Here are some flowers for you to complete. Fill in as much detail as you can on the sketch, then draw the flower again focusing on the outline and simple shapes.

Explore the form in your first drawing and then simplify in your second try.

2 Now do the same for some plants.

76

3 And some shells on a seashore.

4 Or rocks in the desert.

I think I'd make quite a good rock.

WARM-UP #7 Just Use Tone

This is where you don't use an outline at all. Choose an object you can see around you, such as a piece of fruit or a pile of books. Simply use areas of light and dark or midtone to capture how your object appears.

It's good to start out really messy here. Try shading a large area of midtone first and then cut into that with your eraser for lights and your dark-coloured pencil for darks.

I really like using chalks, or even mud for doing this kind of drawing.

BIG IDEA #10 Environment

If buildings feel big, then an environment is VAST, but what you actually need to understand is COMPOSITION. This is how you decide where to put different elements on the page IN RELATION to everything else.

A nicely composed picture draws the viewer in, leads their eye around the picture to the most interesting parts and maybe even tells a story.

I just put what I want to look at in the middle and bite away everything else.

When drawing a landscape, you need to know which part is the most important part to you.

The house in the distance?

The dog asleep in the foreground?

The boats in the midground?

80

Once you know which part is top priority, you can highlight this by using various techniques.

Use contrast (light or dark areas) to draw attention to what you want the viewer to look at first.

Leading lines draw the eye into the picture from the edges.

If you combine both elements, you will make sure that the viewer focuses on what is important to you.

ACTIVITY #24

1 What could you add to this picture to make the car the centre of attention?

Other than me, of course!

Different landscapes have their own challenges.

Mountains are often very far away so you need to work out how to show that distance.

Deserts are flat and often don't have a lot of elements to illustrate.

Forests can almost have too much detail with many leaves, branches or trees to draw.

Water is almost always moving. How do you show that in your picture?

If drawing from a photo or real life, you can decide what to include and what to leave out, if it makes a better picture.

82

ACTIVITY #24

1 Superdog saves the day again. This time you choose the environment. Is Superdog in nature, a city, the desert or at the North Pole?

My cousin told me that if you draw something wonky, the art police come and take away your pencils... But he also lives in a sewer, so we don't listen to my cousin.

Just like with anatomy drawing, once you know the principles of composition, you can start sticking ideas together to make new, fantasy worlds.

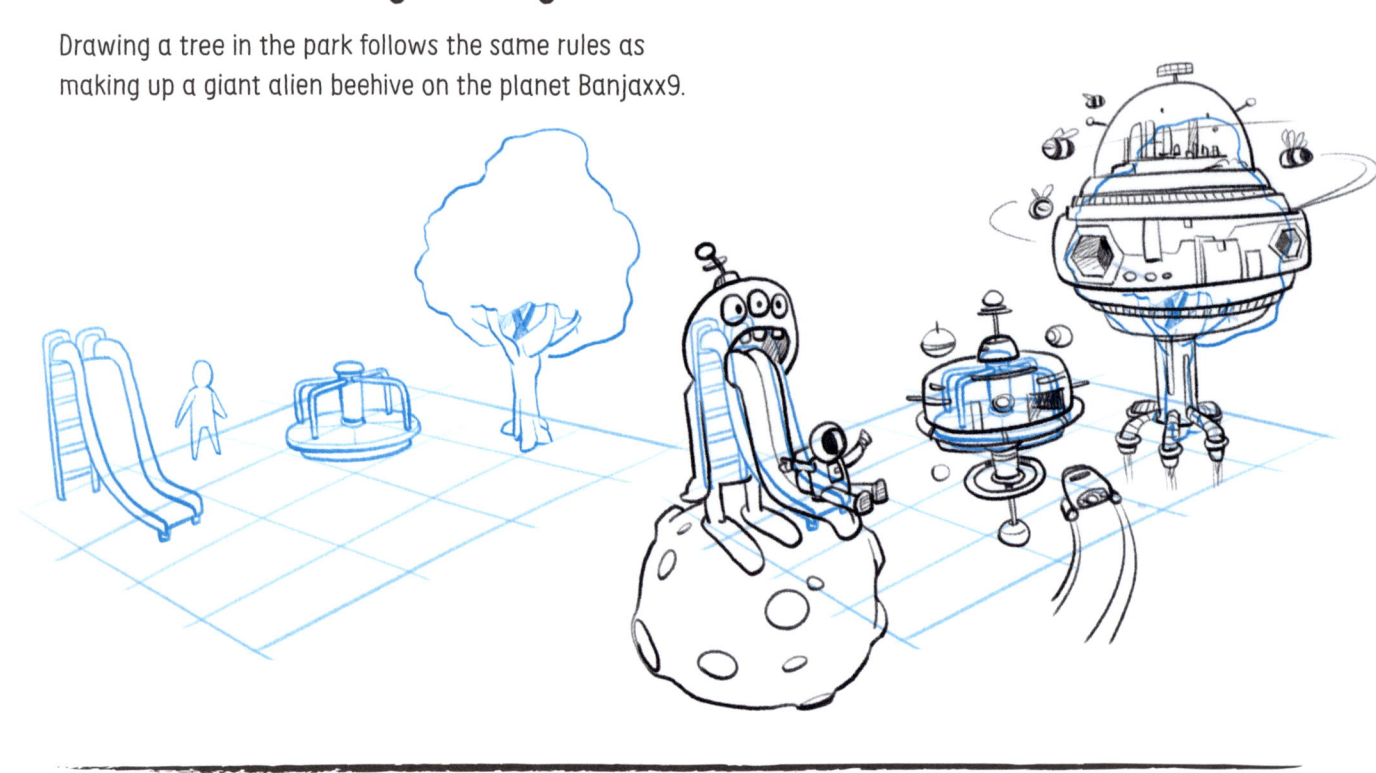

Drawing a tree in the park follows the same rules as making up a giant alien beehive on the planet Banjaxx9.

If you can draw furniture or buildings, you can create your own ALIEN WORLD. It's simply about applying the BIG IDEA and adding in the details.

Before you start, take some time deciding what your view will be. Most of drawing is just thoughtful seeing.

84

ACTIVITY #25

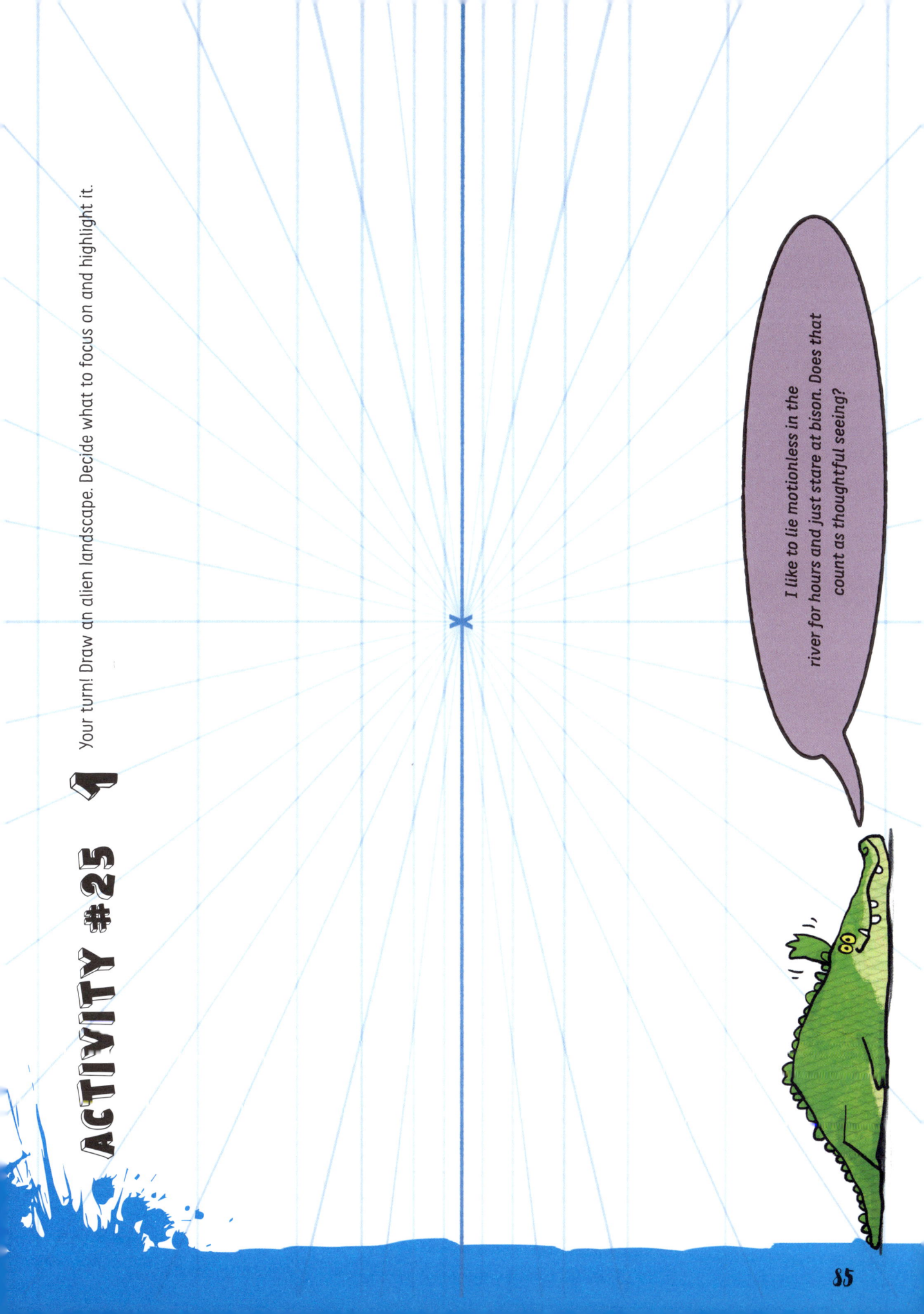

1 Your turn! Draw an alien landscape. Decide what to focus on and highlight it.

I like to lie motionless in the river for hours and just stare at bison. Does that count as thoughtful seeing?

85

So Can You Draw?

Well done for getting this far.

You have learned how to use tone and shade. You know what perspective really does and how to combine it with tone to create realistic 3D objects on a page.

You know how to draw humans and animals, as well as aliens, dinosaurs and any other creature that comes to mind.

Honestly, some of these sketches were just fabulous, darling!

You know how to show expression through eyes, mouths and hands, as well as posture and action.

Some mouths are easier than others, though.

You've tackled vehicles, buildings, nature and landscapes.

And you know what to put in as well as what to leave out.

You've practised blind drawing, quick drawing, one-line drawing and many other warm-ups to get you ready for all those BIG IDEAS.

Wow, we're all really good at drawing. What shall we draw next?

Congratulations! You can draw!

Perspective Grids

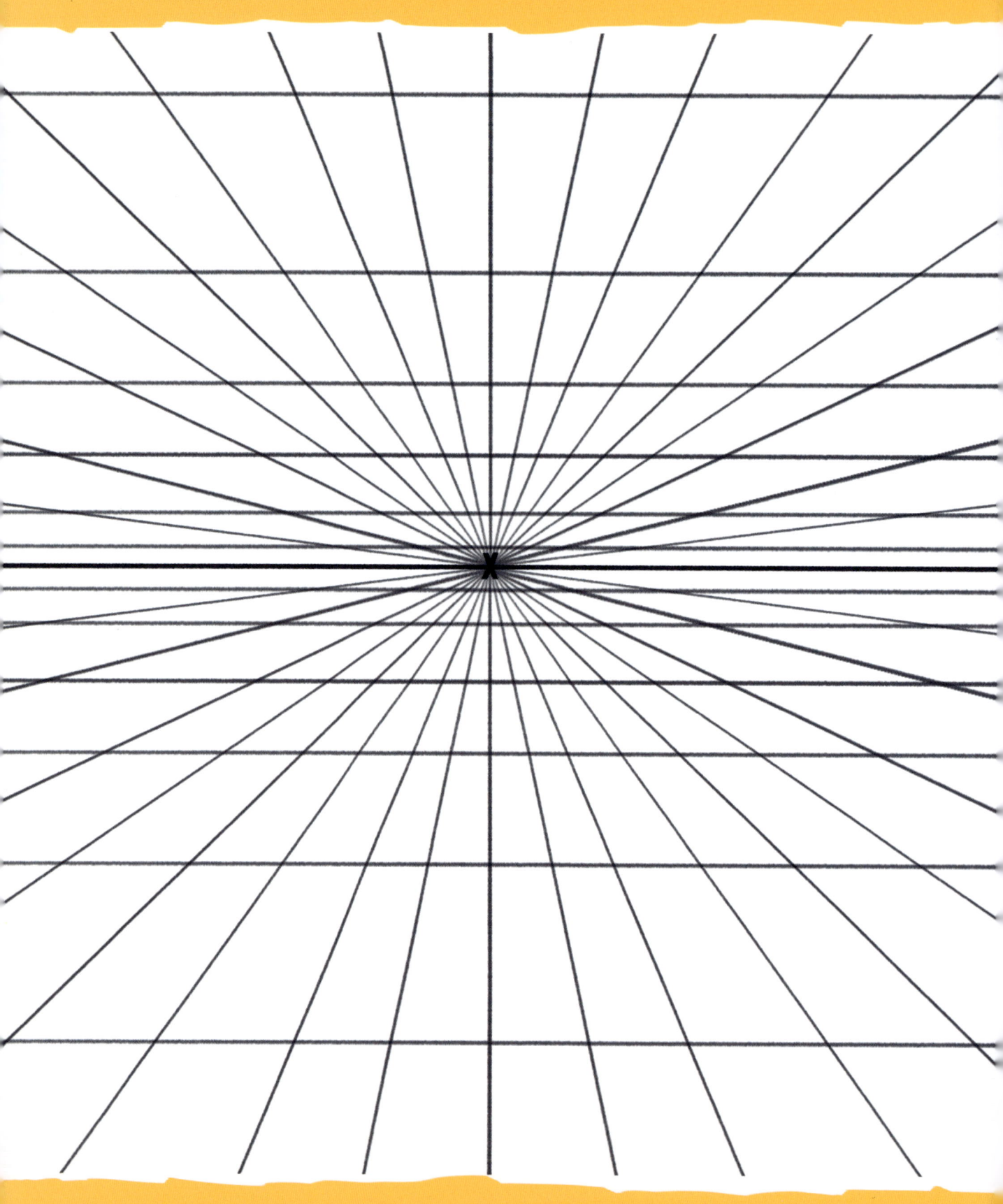

89

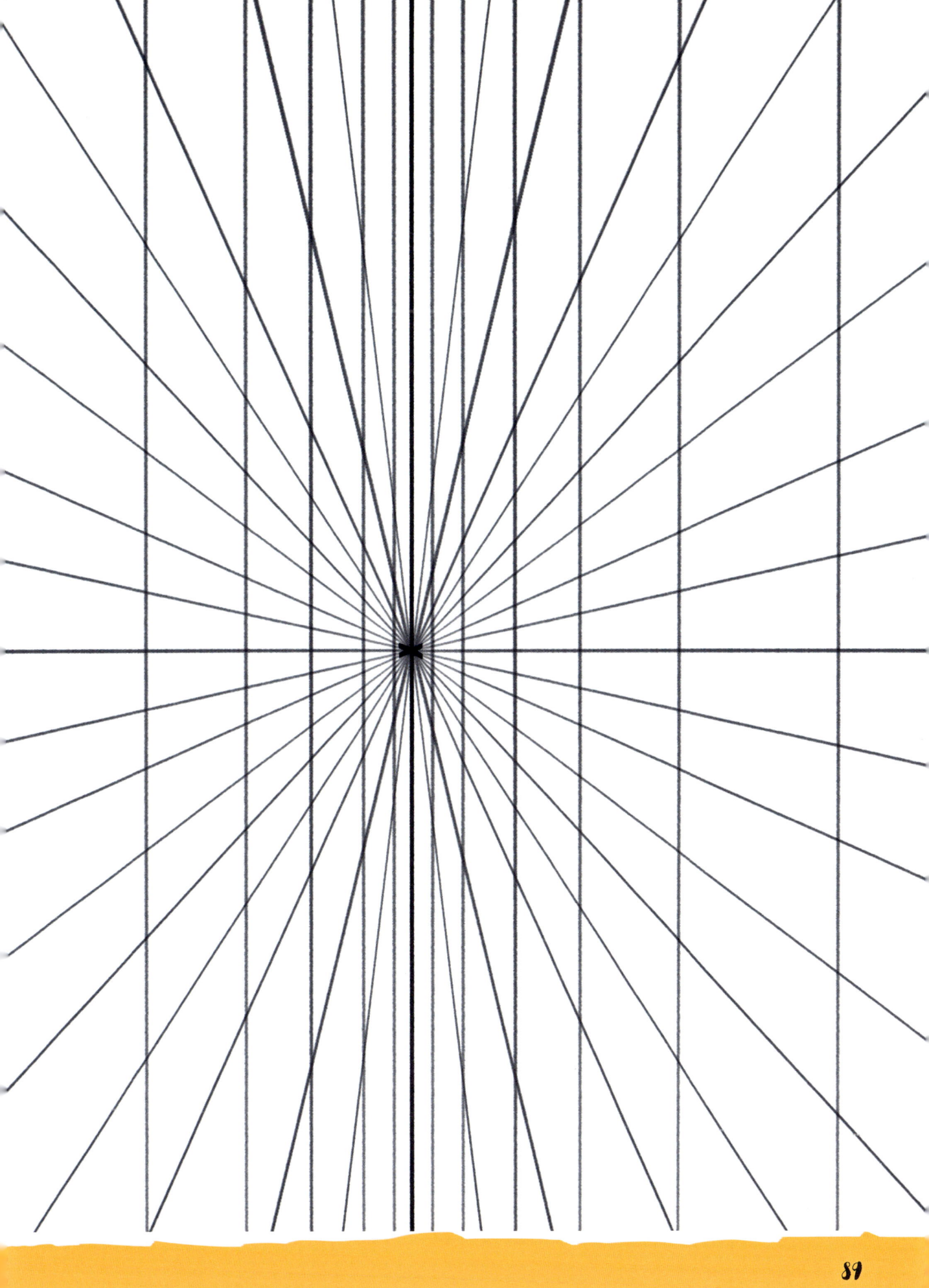

Practice Pages

Here are some blank pages for you to practise your new drawing skills!

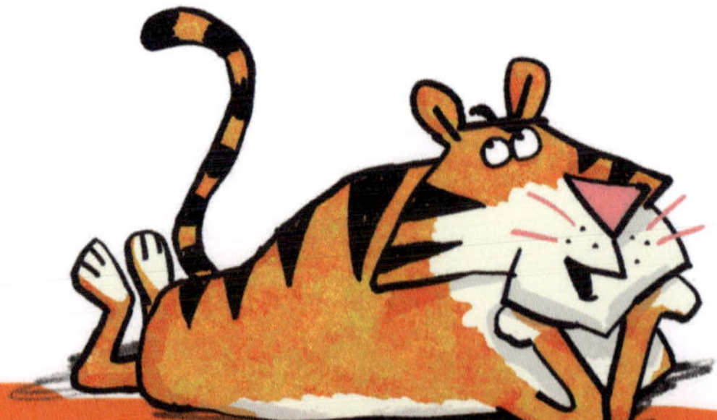

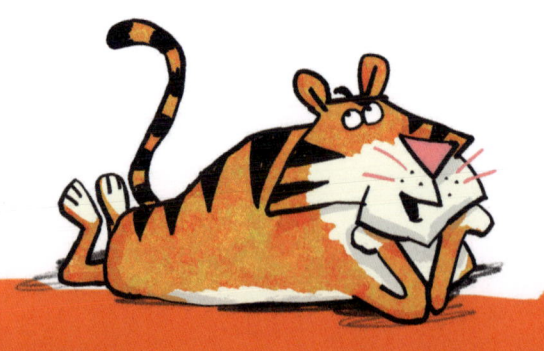

Index

A
aliens, 58, 84
animals, 54–59
    core shapes, 58
    extinct and fantasy creatures, 56–57
    insects, 58
    mammals, 54–56
    sea creatures, 58
    skeletons, 54–55, 58

B
blending, 16
blind drawing, 42–43
buildings, 68–71
    centre of gravity line, 70
    fantasy buildings, 70
    grids, 69
    outlines, 68
    scale, 68

C
cars, 62–63
cartoon characters, 29, 40
centre of gravity line, 70
circles, 10–11
colour pencils, 6
composition, 80, 84
contrast, 48, 81
creative block, 32

D
depth, 24, 29
deserts, 82

E
environment, 80–85
    composition, 80, 84
    fantasy worlds, 84
    landscape, 80–82
equipment, 6–7
eraser, 7
expression, 7, 36, 38, 40, 44–51
eyeline, 22, 23, 25
eyes, 46–47, 50

F
faces, 44–51
    asymmetry, 49
    character and expression, 7, 36, 38, 40, 44–51
    eyes, 46–47, 50
    mouths, 48–49, 50
    movement, 44
    proportions, 44
fantasy worlds, 84
flowers, 76
foreshortening, 24
forests, 82

G
grids, 69

H
hand poses, 40–41
horizon, 20, 22, 29
human body, 7, 34–39, 54
    action poses, 38, 39
    balance, 38
    posture, 36, 37, 38
    static poses, 38
    see also **people**

L
landscape, 80–82
    deserts, 82
    forests, 82
    mountains, 82
    water, 82
leading lines, 81
light and shade, 12–17, 26, 28, 30, 31, 78
line-edge quality, 52–53, 63

M
mid-midtones, 12, 14
midtones, 12, 13, 14, 31, 78
mirror, 7
mountains, 82
mouths, 48–49, 50
movement, 34, 35, 38, 44

N
nature, 74–77
    flowers, 76
    plants, 76
    rocks, 77
    shells, 77
    trees, 74–75, 82

O
one-line drawing, 60–61
overlap, 24, 29, 31, 35

P
paper, 7
pencils, 6
people, 34–39
    faces, 44–51
    hand poses, 40–41
perspective, 7, 20–25, 29, 31
photos, drawing from, 82
plants, 76

Q
quick drawing, 66–67

R
rocks, 77
ruler, 7

S
scribble monsters, 72–73
shells, 77
squinting, 12, 74
straight lines, 8–9

T
3D objects, 12, 16, 28
thumb measuring, 18–19
tone, 6, 12–17, 29, 31, 78–79
    blending, 16
    mid-midtones, 12, 14
    midtones, 12, 13, 14, 31, 78
    tonal range, 12
trees, 74–75, 82
two-minute triples, 26–27

V
vanishing point, 20, 21, 23, 25, 28
vehicles, 62–65
    cars, 62–63
    trucks, 64
verb-noun raffle, 32–33

W
water, 82

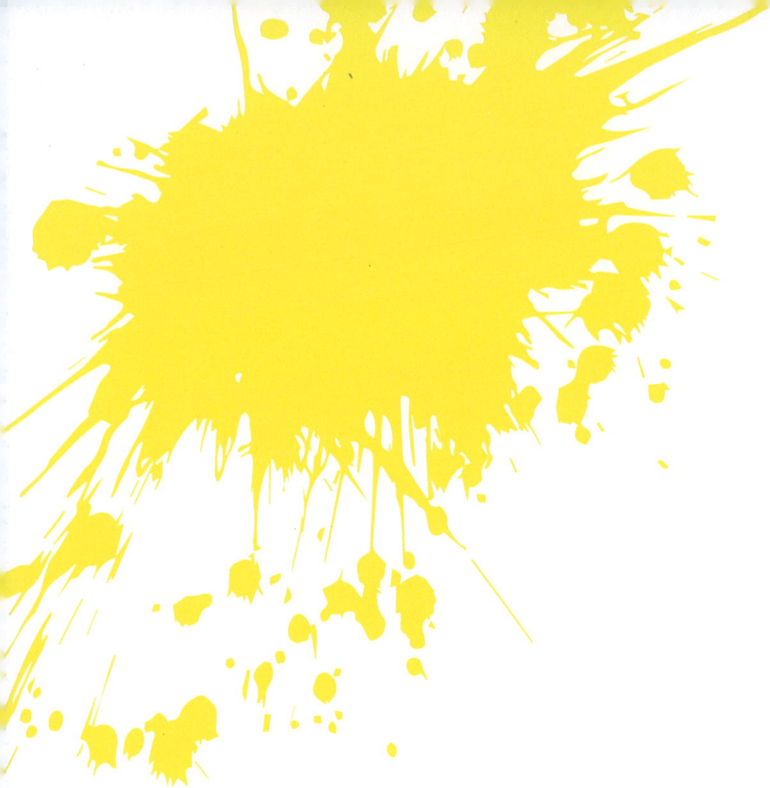

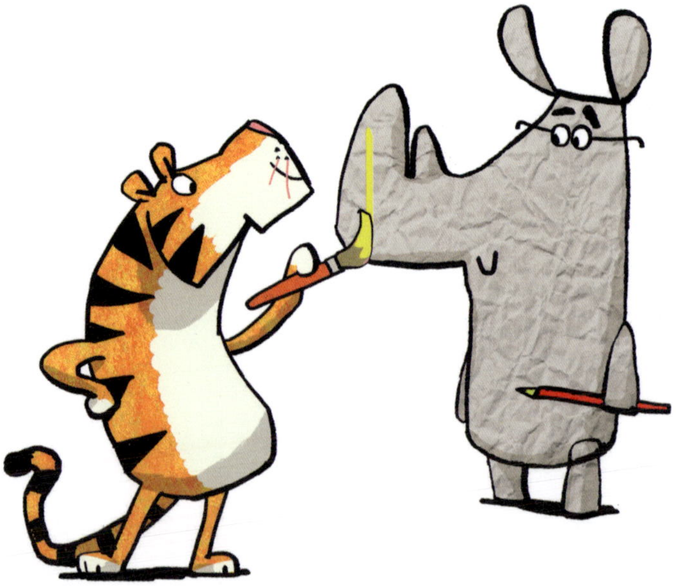